# Police Accountability

## Civilian Advisory and Review Boards in North Carolina Local Government

John B. Stephens

The School of Government at the University of North Carolina at Chapel Hill works to improve the lives of North Carolinians by engaging in practical scholarship that helps public officials and citizens understand and improve state and local government. Established in 1931 as the Institute of Government, the School provides educational, advisory, and research services for state and local governments. The School of Government is also home to a nationally ranked Master of Public Administration program, the North Carolina Judicial College, and specialized centers focused on community and economic development, information technology, and environmental finance.

As the largest university-based local government training, advisory, and research organization in the United States, the School of Government offers up to 200 courses, webinars, and specialized conferences for more than 12,000 public officials each year. In addition, faculty members annually publish approximately 50 books, manuals, reports, articles, bulletins, and other print and online content related to state and local government. The School also produces the *Daily Bulletin Online* each day the General Assembly is in session, reporting on activities for members of the legislature and others who need to follow the course of legislation.

Operating support for the School of Government's programs and activities comes from many sources, including state appropriations, local government membership dues, private contributions, publication sales, course fees, and service contracts.

Visit sog.unc.edu or call 919.966.5381 for more information on the School's courses, publications, programs, and services.

Michael R. Smith, DEAN
Aimee N. Wall, SENIOR ASSOCIATE DEAN
Jennifer Willis, ASSOCIATE DEAN FOR DEVELOPMENT
Michael Vollmer, ASSOCIATE DEAN FOR ADMINISTRATION

## FACULTY

Whitney Afonso
Trey Allen (on leave)
Gregory S. Allison
Lydian Altman
David N. Ammons
Maureen Berner
Frayda S. Bluestein
Kirk Boone
Mark F. Botts
Anita R. Brown-Graham
Peg Carlson
Connor Crews
Leisha DeHart-Davis
Shea Riggsbee Denning
Sara DePasquale
Jacquelyn Greene
Margaret F. Henderson

Norma Houston (on leave)
Cheryl Daniels Howell
Willow S. Jacobson
James L. Joyce
Robert P. Joyce
Diane M. Juffras
Dona G. Lewandowski
Adam Lovelady
James M. Markham
Christopher B. McLaughlin
Kara A. Millonzi
Jill D. Moore
Jonathan Q. Morgan
Ricardo S. Morse
C. Tyler Mulligan
Kimberly L. Nelson
Kristi A. Nickodem

David W. Owens
Obed Pasha
William C. Rivenbark
Dale J. Roenigk
John Rubin
Jessica Smith
Meredith Smith
Carl W. Stenberg III
John B. Stephens
Charles Szypszak
Thomas H. Thornburg
Shannon H. Tufts
Emily Turner
Jeffrey B. Welty (on leave)
Richard B. Whisnant
Brittany L. Williams

25 24 23 22 21    1 2 3 4 5
ISBN 978-1-64238-029-3

# Contents

## Appendix B
## Additional Resources    73

# Acknowledgments

I am pleased to thank several people and organizations for their contributions to this book. First, I want to thank the many local government officials and citizens serving on civilian advisory (CABs) and/or review boards (CRBs) for information about their respective jurisdictions' experience with CABs and CRBs.

I appreciate the assistance of Fred Baggett, Legislative Counsel for the N.C. Association of Chiefs of Police, in identifying jurisdictions with experience of CABs and CRBs. I thank Nikki Abija for researching and authoring the CAB/CRB profiles of Asheville, Charlotte, Greenville, and Winston-Salem (Appendix A), and for providing input on comparisons among all the profiled CABs and CRBs. Finally, thanks to my University of North Carolina at Chapel Hill School of Government colleagues, Hana Haidar, Kevin Justice, Robby Poore, and Emily Hinkle, for their excellent work and patience in managing late changes in content and their expert design and layout.

# Preface

The relationship between law enforcement agencies and the communities they serve is the foundation for issues that are raising strong feelings. Changing philosophies, strategies, and tactics of policing significantly impact all residents of a jurisdiction. Dramatic instances of the use of force by police have prompted protests from large numbers of people in the United States and beyond.

What elected officials and other citizens understand about policing, how they compare their expectations for community-police interactions to their experiences, and how they evaluate claims of police misconduct in their communities are top-line concerns in many places. Questions of appropriate transparency and accountability, balanced with upholding professional standards and practices of policing, as well as protecting active investigations, draw great attention and debate.

North Carolina cities and counties utilize appointed advisory boards to guide many government functions. My previous work on such advisory bodies prompted me to research the advisory body form of community engagement with, and oversight of, law enforcement in the state.

Many factors affect trust in and perceptions of equity in policing practices. This book seeks to provide a starting point for North Carolina public leaders to examine the forms of civilian oversight and advice to law enforcement agencies.

Chapter 1

# Police Accountability through Civilian Advisory and Review Boards

## Introduction

The role of community members in influencing policing policies and practices has gained more attention in recent years. Criticisms of racial profiling and improper use of force, as well as perceptions of inadequate investigation and discipline of officer conduct, have prompted questions about the best forms of police accountability for local government.[1]

This book examines civilian advisory and review boards[2] as forms of input for or oversight of police departments and sheriffs' offices in North Carolina. It aims to assist law enforcement leaders, local government officials, and concerned community members in understanding the goals of such advisory and review bodies. By describing several policing advisory and review bodies in North Carolina local government,[3] including their powers and responsibilities, membership, types of activities, and work outputs, this book informs local government practice and policy choices on civilian-based approaches to police accountability.

---

1. In North Carolina, local law enforcement includes county sheriffs, who are elected, and municipal police departments, which are overseen by an elected body. In this book, the terms *police* and *officers* also refer to sheriffs and deputies.

2. Civilian advisory boards and civilian review boards are also known as *citizen advisory boards* and *citizen review boards*, respectively. The terms *civilian* and *citizen* are used interchangeably in this book, and both terms refer to non-police officers. Note that in the context of police advisory and review bodies, the term *citizen* does not relate to an individual's status of citizenship in the United States. Civilian advisory boards can also be called *citizen/civilian advisory committees*, and civilian review boards can also be called *citizen/civilian review committees*. Note also that *community* is sometimes used in lieu of *citizen* or *civilian*, meaning that the acronym "CRB" can refer to a "citizen/civilian" review board or a "community" citizen/civilian review board. Similarly, the acronym "CAB" can refer to a "citizen/civilian" advisory board or a "community" advisory board.

3. Civilian review boards exercise powers related to police department investigations and disciplinary actions on officers or analyze patterns of policing for matters of fairness and effectiveness. Civilian advisory boards do not have internally focused duties, but offer voices, ideas, and guidance from community members and often work with law enforcement leaders in outreach and education efforts. See the "Models of Civilian Oversight of and Advice to North Carolina Local Law Enforcement" section of this chapter for a complete description of civilian review boards and civilian advisory boards.

There are five common goals of civilian oversight of law enforcement. Based on a review of ninety-seven civilian oversight programs, the National Association for Civilian Oversight of Law Enforcement (NACOLE) found that the following aspirations were the most common among these programs:

a. improving public trust;
b. ensuring accessible complaint processes;
c. promoting thorough, fair investigations;
d. increasing transparency; and
e. deterring police misconduct.[12]

NACOLE explains two other ways that civilian oversight can help. One, "[c]ivilian oversight is a developing area of civil rights protection," in that civilian oversight programs' work on auditing individual cases or examining possible patterns could identify civil rights violations.[13] Second, NACOLE believes that oversight helps manage a "municipality's exposure to risk from lawsuits claiming unlawful actions by individual officers or departmental failures to supervise or train officers." Civilian oversight can range from reviewing individual cases of alleged misconduct to evaluating police management, supervision, and training.[14]

Additional purposes of civilian oversight of law enforcement are associated more with civilian advisory bodies, which do not focus on individual complaints about police conduct. Rather, these bodies focus on creating and maintaining positive police-community relations, acting as a liaison for community concerns, and providing input on police policies and steps for departments that choose to pursue accreditation with a state or national body.[15]

## Models of Civilian Oversight of and Advice to North Carolina Local Law Enforcement

The description and analysis of civilian involvement in police conduct usually center on accountability of individual cases of officer-citizen interactions and

12. Joseph De Angelis, Richard Rosenthal, and Brian Buchner, *Civilian Oversight of Law Enforcement: A Review of the Strengths and Weaknesses of Various Models* (Tucson, AZ: National Association for Civilian Oversight of Law Enforcement, 2016), 8, https://d3n8a8pro7vhmx.cloudfront.net/nacole/pages/161/attachments/original/1481727977/NACOLE_short_doc_FINAL.pdf?1481727977.

13. "Civilian Oversight Basics: Civilian Oversight 101," National Association for Civilian Oversight of Law Enforcement, accessed March 8, 2021, https://www.nacole.org/civilian_oversight_basics.

14. Ibid.

15. For example, North Carolina Law Enforcement Accreditation administered by the North Carolina Department of Justice (https://ncdoj.gov/north-carolina-law-enforcement-accreditation/) and national accreditation from the Commission on Accreditation for Law Enforcement Agencies, Inc. (CALEA) (https://www.calea.org/).

general patterns of policing. Three models of oversight are commonly cited. In this book, a fourth model is added to categorize the government-appointed entities in North Carolina that have responsibilities other than addressing complaints regarding individual officer conduct or specific civilian-police interactions.

## Three Models of Oversight

There have been different "civilian oversight classification systems developed over the years because of the wide variation in approaches adopted by communities."[16] The National Association for Civilian Oversight of Law Enforcement (NACOLE) adopted a system developed in 2001,[17] with some modifications. NACOLE places civilian oversight bodies in one of three classifications:

1. **The investigation-focused model** involves routine, independent investigations of complaints against police officers, which may replace or duplicate police internal affairs processes, though non-police civilian investigators staff them.
2. **The review-focused model** concentrates on commenting on completed investigations after reviewing the quality of police internal affairs investigations. Recommendations may be made to police executives regarding findings, or there may be a request that further investigations be conducted. A review board composed of citizen volunteers commonly heads this model, and they may hold public meetings to collect community input and facilitate police-community communication.
3. **The auditor/monitor model** focuses on examining broad patterns in complaint investigations including patterns in the quality of investigations, findings, and discipline rendered. Further, in some cities that use this model, auditor/monitors may actively participate in or monitor open internal investigations. This model often seeks to promote broad organizational change by conducting systematic reviews of police policies, practices or training, and making recommendations for improvement.[18]

The characteristics, strengths, and weaknesses of each of these models are presented in the report, "Civilian Oversight of Law Enforcement: A Review of the Strengths and Weaknesses of Various Models" (2016).[19] Even with the three categories of civilian oversight bodies, the authors caution that there is high variability in organizational structure, wide differences in organizational authority, and several instances of organizational "hybrids."[20] Similarly, a 2018

---

16. Stephens, Scrivner, and Cambareri, *Civilian Oversight of the Police*, 1.

17. Samuel Walker, *Police Accountability: The Role of Citizen Oversight* (Belmont, CA: Wadsworth/Thomson, 2001).

18. Stephens, Scrivner, and Cambareri, *Civilian Oversight*, 1 (drawing from Joseph De Angelis, Richard Rosenthal, and Brian Buchner's *Civilian Oversight of Law Enforcement: Assessing the Evidence*).

19. See De Angelis, Rosenthal, and Buchner, *Strengths and Weaknesses*.

20. Ibid., 6.

study of civilian oversight bodies in major cities in the United States and Canada notes that "[c]ivilian oversight programs vary significantly from one city to the next and even within the general categories . . . and in some communities there are aspects of all of the models."[21]

## A Fourth Model: Advisory

An additional category is needed when examining government-appointed bodies for community input on policing in North Carolina. An **advisory** civilian body has formal appointments by one or more local officials and can focus on a range of topics in policing and public safety.

Advisory bodies vary in scope of work. General goals and activities center on informational, educational, or "community voice" duties for providing input to their respective jurisdictions' law enforcement leaders. Some examples of the goals and activities of advisory bodies are the following:

- enhance police/community relations, communications, transparency, and community confidence;[22]
- promote educational, outreach activities to increase public safety awareness;[23]
- communicate information about the police department and its goals to the citizens that are served, along with media inquiries as appropriate;[24]
- serve as a liaison between the community and city council;[25]
- assist in developing programs and projects to foster communication with various disproportionately affected groups;[26]
- help build trust and relationships between the police department and the community;[27]
- offer recommendations to the police chief regarding services and practices;[28] and
- assist with reviews of police departments' citizen police academy curricula.[29]

---

21. Stephens, Scrivner, and Cambareri, *Civilian Oversight of the Police*, 2.

22. The City of Salisbury, North Carolina, *Charter of the Salisbury Police Department Police Chief's Citizen Advisory Board* (2018), 1.

23. "Community Policing Advisory Board," Town of Knightdale, North Carolina, accessed May 20, 2021, https://www.knightdalenc.gov/government/advisory-boards/community-policing-advisory-board.

24. Town of Spencer, North Carolina, *Spencer Police Department Police Chief's Citizen Advisory Board Charter* (2021), 3.

25. "Police Advisory Board," Raleigh, North Carolina, accessed May 20, 2021, https://raleighnc.gov/police-advisory-board.

26. Town of Spencer, North Carolina, *Citizen Advisory Board Charter*.

27. Raleigh, North Carolina, "Police Advisory Board."

28. Town of Knightdale, North Carolina, "Community Policing Advisory Board."

29. Ibid.

The main distinction between all three models of civilian oversight bodies and civilian advisory bodies is that civilian advisory bodies are not empowered to conduct monitoring, review, or investigations of police conduct. To specify their limits, bodies in the advisory category do not

- handle individual complaints about police conduct,
- conduct independent investigations,
- review or monitor a police department's handling of complaints, or
- examine possible patterns of policing for improvements.[30]

In this book, the first three models (i.e., the investigation-focused model, the review-focused model, and the auditor/monitor model), discussed in the "Three Models of Oversight" section in this chapter can be understood as citizen review boards (CRBs), or citizen oversight agencies (COAs), and the fourth category refers to citizen advisory boards (CABs).[31]

---

30. There are exceptions, as some civilian advisory boards do carry out these functions.

31. The publications cited in this book use the terms *citizen oversight boards* (COBs) and *citizen oversight agencies* (COAs). COBs and COAs refer to the same kinds of bodies covered in the NACOLE-defined three categories. COBs and COAs are considered citizen review boards (CRBs) in this publication.

## Distinction between Citizen Review Boards/Citizen Oversight Agencies and Citizen Advisory Boards

### Citizen Review Boards or Citizen Oversight Agencies

*Three models, per the National Association for Civilian Oversight of Law Enforcement (NACOLE)*

- **The investigation-focused model** conducts independent investigations of complaints against police officers, which may replace or duplicate police internal affairs processes.
- **The review-focused model** concentrates on commenting on completed investigations after reviewing the quality of police internal affairs investigations with feedback to police executives or a request that further investigations be done.
- **The auditor/monitor model** focuses on examining broad patterns across complaint investigations, including patterns in the quality of investigations, findings, and discipline rendered.

Typically appointed by local government elected body

Access to sensitive or confidential information for case review or investigation

### Citizen Advisory Boards

*Various "input" and "community voice" to local law enforcement; varied duties and scope of work*

**General goals:**
- Improve community interactions and relationships with the police
- Promote educational and outreach activities to increase public safety awareness
- Serve as a liaison between the community and city council and/or police department

**Targeted activities:**
- Convene community forums on policing
- Assist in developing programs and projects to foster communication with various disproportionately affected groups
- Offer recommendations to the police chief about policies and practices
- Assist with the reviews of police departments' citizen police academy curricula

Appointed by town manager, police chief/sheriff, or elected body

Does not do individual case review or investigation

*Source:* Joseph De Angelis, Richard Rosenthal, and Brian Buchner, *Civilian Oversight of Law Enforcement: A Review of the Strengths and Weaknesses of Various Models* (National Association for Civilian Oversight of Law Enforcement, OJP Diagnostic Center, and U.S. Department of Justice, 2016) (left column); John B. Stephens, summarizing the "A Fourth Model: Advisory" section in Chapter 1 of this book (right column).

# Chapter 2

# Civilian Advisory and Review Boards: Motivating Factors, Formation, and Management

## Factors Contributing to Interest in Civilian Advisory (CABs) and Review Boards (CRBs)

At least three concerns draw attention to the possible benefits of civilian advisory (CABs) and review boards (CRBs):

a. the persistent gap of confidence or trust in police by people of color,
b. proposals to reform or strengthen police actions where there is risk of negative impact on a suspect or community, and
c. a heightened focus on police accountability and improving community views of police.

According to the 2020 report of the North Carolina Task Force for Racial Equity in Criminal Justice (NCTFRECJ), "[g]enerally speaking, Black Americans do not engage with or trust the police as much as other communities."[1] National polls, such as Gallup, provide details of this skepticism or distrust.

Gallup polling has tracked perceptions of fairness and levels of trust in law enforcement of white and black respondents since 1986. In 2020, Gallup found that "[f]ifty-six percent of White adults and 19% of Black adults say they have 'a great deal' or 'quite a lot' of confidence in the police. This 37-percentage-point racial gap is the largest found for any of 16 major U.S. institutions rated in Gallup's annual Confidence in Institutions poll."[2]

---

1. North Carolina Task Force for Racial Equity in Criminal Justice (NCTFRECJ), *Task Force for Racial Equity in Criminal Justice: Report 2020* (Raleigh, NC: Office of the Governor, 2020), 13, https://ncdoj.gov/wp-content/uploads/2021/02/TRECReportFinal_02262021.pdf. (The task force was established by Executive Order 145).

2. Jeffrey M. Jones, "Black, White Adults' Confidence Diverges Most on Police," *Gallup*, August 12, 2020. https://news.gallup.com/poll/317114/black-white-adults-confidence-diverges -police.aspx.

Similar findings on confidence in the police were presented in the 2015 final report of the President's Task Force on 21st Century Policing. The survey questions were as follows:

How much confidence do you have in police officers in your community . . .

- . . . to do a good job of enforcing the law?
- . . . to not use excessive force on suspects?
- . . . to treat Hispanics and Whites equally?
- . . . to treat Blacks and Whites equally?[3]

Across each question, white respondents who answered "a great deal" or "a fair amount" of confidence were 72 to 74 percent. This compares to lower confidence from Hispanic respondents (45 to 47 percent) and Black respondents (36 to 41 percent).[4]

In 2020, as part of analyzing possible effects of the coronavirus pandemic on U.S. institutions, Gallup reported that "[a]t the same time that several institutions have engendered greater public confidence, one—the police—stands alone as seeing a significant decline in the past year. Confidence in the police fell five points to 48%, marking the first time in the 27-year trend that this reading is below the majority level."[5] Gallup attributes the drop to "public outcry after George Floyd was killed during an arrest in Minneapolis in late May, which sparked nationwide protests against excessive use of force by the police."[6] The overall public confidence level in police has been as high as 64 percent in the past, according to Gallup.[7]

Polling specific to North Carolina residents is minimal on aspects of police-community relations. An Elon University poll of 799 registered voters occurred following the September 20, 2016, shooting of Keith Lamont Scott by a Charlotte police officer. The poll found that "[a]mong black voters, 82 percent said police treat blacks worse than whites while 33 percent of white voters had the same opinion."[8]

---

3. See Figure 2 (sourced from Pew Research Center) in President's Task Force on 21st Century Policing, *Final Report of the President's Task Force on 21st Century Policing* (Washington, DC: U.S. Department of Justice Office of Community Oriented Policing Services, 2015), 13, https://cops.usdoj.gov/pdf/taskforce/taskforce_finalreport.pdf.

4. Ibid., 9–10.

5. Megan Brenan, "Amid Pandemic, Confidence in Key U.S. Institutions Surges," *Gallup*, August 12, 2020, https://news.gallup.com/poll/213869/confidence-police-back-historical -average.aspx.

6. Ibid.

7. Ibid.

8. Owen Covington, "ELON POLL: N.C. Voters Split on Police Treatment of Blacks, Support Public Access to Police Videos," *Elon University: Today at Elon*, October 4, 2016, https://www.elon.edu/u/news/2016/10/04/elon-poll-n-c-voters-split-on-police-treatment-of-blacks-support-public-access-to-police-videos/.

## Proposals to Reform Policing

In 2015, the President's Task Force on 21st Century Policing summarized its recommendations under six pillars for effective policing. Pillar Two is "Policy and Oversight." It calls for "[l]aw enforcement agencies [to] collaborate with community members, especially in communities and neighborhoods disproportionately affected by crime, to develop policies and strategies for deploying resources that aim to reduce crime by improving relationships, increasing community engagement, and fostering cooperation."[9]

In addition to recommending transparency concerning data and policies, as well as clear procedures for internal (and some external) review of use of force, the task force explains that "[s]ome form of civilian oversight of law enforcement is important in order to strengthen trust with the community. Every community should define the appropriate form and structure of civilian oversight to meet the needs of that community."[10] The task force calls for police employees to provide input to any consideration of new or additional civilian oversight.

Focusing on effective community engagement, the International Association of Chiefs of Police in 2018 conducted a study of "community participation and leadership" in policing.[11] Among the instances of promising practices in several communities, two CAB/CRBs were profiled:

- the Albany (New York) Community Police Advisory Committee and the Citizens' Police Review Board,[12] and
- Louisville (Kentucky) Citizens Commission on Police Accountability and Training Advisory Board.[13]

In June 2020, North Carolina Governor Roy Cooper formed the North Carolina Task Force for Racial Equity in Criminal Justice (NCTFRECJ). The NCTFRECJ issued its final report in December 2020. At the general level of community-police relations, the NCTFRECJ called for a recommitment to "community policing as an agency-wide philosophy" and that community policing plans be created in "collaboration with the communities they serve." The report explains that this "requires developing and cultivating trusted relationships between members of the community and law enforcement officers and meeting regularly with those liaisons and other community members."[14]

---

9. President's Task Force on 21st Century Policing, *Final Report*, 19.

10. President's Task Force on 21st Century Policing, *Final Report*, 26.

11. International Association of Chiefs of Police, *Practices in Modern Policing, Community Participation and Leadership* (Alexandria, VA: International Association of Chiefs of Police, 2018), https://www.theiacp.org/sites/default/files/2018-11/IACP_PMP_Community%20 Leadership.pdf.

12. Ibid., 5–8.

13. Ibid., 15–16.

14. NCTFRECJ, *Report 2020*, 28.

The NCTFRECJ also offered recommendations to "[i]mprove law enforcement accountability and culture."[15] Specific to bodies for civilian oversight, they asserted that "[a]t present, North Carolina has few civilian oversight boards, and those that exist have very little meaningful authority. This hampers the extent to which these boards can serve as true instruments of accountability."[16]

The section of the NCTFRECJ's report on improving local civilian oversight boards (COBs) makes several recommendations, including the suggestion that local governments aiming to form COBs "coordinate with NACOLE regarding best practices and necessary policies and procedures" and that state laws should be revised to allow for "inspection of certain records related to internal investigations by COBs and local governing bodies."[17]

Further specifying the access and use of such records, the NCTFRECJ calls for restrictions on the use of and access to "COBs created by a local government, or the local government governing body" and calls for the creation of a legal distinction "between the documents used in the investigation of the incident and the ultimate disposition or personnel action, which would remain a part of the personnel file and therefore be unavailable to COBs." Moreover, the NCTFRECJ explains that records related to internal investigations by COBs "are not public records with the exception of aggregated use of force data."[18]

For COB operations, the NCTFRECJ explains that "COBs or local government council or commission" should be allowed to review "documents related to the internal affairs investigation" by these bodies, but COBs and/or local government should not be allowed "to have copies or further release these documents or the information contained therein."[19]

Once a COB review is complete, NCTFRECJ believes that the COB should be empowered to "[r]ecommend that the agency involved in the inquiry take certain steps to address the incident," and "[r]ecommend that the Standards Commissions[20] review certain incidents for compliance with requirements of the NCAC [N.C. Administrative Code]," contingent on funding.[21]

---

15. Ibid., 52–60.

16. Ibid., 52.

17. Ibid., 53–54.

18. Ibid., 54.

19. Ibid.

20. "Standards Commissions" refers to the "North Carolina Criminal Justice Education and Training Standards Commission" and "North Carolina Sheriffs' Education and Training Standards Commission."

21. NCTFRECJ, *Report 2020*, 54.

## Guidance on Forming and Managing CABs and CRBs

As noted above, due to the various models of CABs and CRBs, there is no uniform guidance on how to form and operate these bodies. The National Association for Civilian Oversight of Law Enforcement (NACOLE) notes that "[t]here is no right answer as to what an effective police oversight body 'must' look like."[22]

Similarly, a recent analysis of five large cities in Texas with versions of CRBs, explains that "[t]he five police departments in this report all have different issues; they also have different issues compared to those in Texas's rural cities, college towns or border metropolises. Their civilian oversight agencies should, accordingly, have some different functions."[23]

There are a few pointers for creating CABs and CRBs from relevant sources. In 2020, drawing from earlier work and resources, NACOLE summarized thirteen guiding principles for effective civilian oversight agencies.

NACOLE states, "[t]ogether, these 13 principles form the preconditions for effective civilian oversight of law enforcement. However, building effective oversight requires balancing and prioritizing these principles, based on what stakeholders determine to be most important for the community the agency serves."[24] The thirteen principles for CRBs laid out by NACOLE are as follows:

1. independence;
2. clearly defined and adequate jurisdiction and authority;
3. unfettered access to records and facilities;
4. access to law enforcement executives and internal affairs staff;
5. full cooperation with staff;
6. sustained stakeholder support;
7. adequate funding and resources;
8. public reporting and transparency;
9. policy and pattern analysis;
10. community outreach;
11. community involvement;
12. confidentiality, anonymity, and protection from retaliation; and
13. procedural justice and legitimacy.[25]

---

22. Brian Buchner et al. (editors), *Guidebook for the Implementation of New or Revitalized Police Oversight* (Tucson, AZ: National Association for Civilian Oversight of Law Enforcement, 2016), 38.

23. Stephen Averill Sherman and William Fulton, *Who's Policing the Police?: A Comparison of the Civilian Agencies that Perform Oversight of Police in Texas' Five Largest Cities* (Houston, TX: Rice University Kinder Institute for Urban Research, 2020), 2.

24. National Association for Civilian Oversight of Law Enforcement (NACOLE), *Thirteen Principles for Effective Oversight* (2020), https://www.lwm-info.org/DocumentCenter/View/4219/13-NACOLE-Thirteen-Principles_PrePublication_Summary.

25. Ibid.

## Comparing the Three CRB Models

NACOLE offers an assessment of the three categories of civilian oversight models.[26] It delineates "potential key strengths" and "potential key weaknesses" of three models of citizen review boards: the investigation-focused, review-focused, and audit/monitor models.[27]

NACOLE's dimensions on strengths and limitations range from cost to possible duplication to the potential to reduce bias and increase community trust. A civilian oversight program's degree of independence is an important factor across many particular strengths and weaknesses. NACOLE's analysis addresses the trade-offs of having volunteers versus paid staff operate the different models, including a focus on specific complaints and cases compared to patterns that may give rise to systemic reform.[28] "There is no one-size-fits-all approach to police oversight. . . . The 'best' approach continues to be a subject of debate. In part, this is because so many different factors influence what particular agencies and communities need and can sustain."[29]

NACOLE concludes its analysis of CRBs with an important cautionary point. From NACOLE's review of thirty years of local experimentation and data from ninety-seven civilian oversight agencies, the report "does not answer two fundamental questions: 'Which forms of oversight are most effective? Under what circumstances should a jurisdiction implement a review-focused model of oversight as opposed to an investigative or auditor/monitor-focused model?'"[30]

Although the answers to those questions are not clear, communities can follow general advice regarding civilian oversight programs, such as that offered by De Angelis, Rosenthal, and Buchner in their report, "Civilian Oversight of Law Enforcement: Assessing the Evidence" (2016). The authors suggest that, when considering how to structure civilian oversight in their communities, jurisdictions should focus on "best fit" rather than "best practices," and the oversight that is established should employ the "least force" necessary to accomplish its goals. The authors also mention several resources that jurisdictions can consult in their consideration of implementing new oversight or reforming current oversight frameworks.[31]

---

26. Joseph De Angelis, Richard Rosenthal, and Brian Buchner, *Civilian Oversight of Law Enforcement: Assessing the Evidence* (National Association for Civilian Oversight of Law Enforcement, OJP Diagnostic Center, and U.S. Department of Justice, 2016), 3, https://d3n8a8pro7vhmx.cloudfront.net/nacole/pages/161/attachments/original/1481727974/NACOLE_AccessingtheEvidence_Final.pdf?1481727974.

27. Joseph De Angelis, Richard Rosenthal, and Brian Buchner, *Civilian Oversight of Law Enforcement: A Review of the Strengths and Weaknesses of Various Models* (Tucson, AZ: National Association for Civilian Oversight of Law Enforcement, 2016), 7–13, https://d3n8a8pro7vhmx.cloudfront.net/nacole/pages/161/.

28. Ibid.

29. Buchner et al., *Guidebook*, 9.

30. De Angelis, Rosenthal, and Buchner, *Assessing the Evidence*, 52.

31. Ibid., 52–53.

The Pennsylvania Commission on Crime and Delinquency (PCCD) cites the three models from the NACOLE study and sets out nine considerations for determining "which model (or hybrid) is best suited for the specific community and law enforcement agencies."[32] The considerations are as follows:

- Determine eligibility criteria for complainants;
- Identify the type(s) of cases to review or investigate;
- Decide where complainants file (i.e., at police station/sheriff's department, directly with oversight program, or another location like city hall);
- Establish extent of openness to public scrutiny (i.e., extent to which hearings, decisions and other deliberations are open to the public and media) as well as reporting procedures (type, content, frequency, distribution);
- Consider whether decisions recommended by the oversight program can be subject to appeal and by whom;
- Determine whether to allow for a mediation option;
- Establish whether to grant subpoena power and/or establish levels of access to police records;
- Identify whether recommendations can be made for findings and/or discipline (in some cases, disciplinary action still falls under the purview of chief and/or sheriff); and
- Address the role of officer legal representation.[33]

The PCCD also states that "[m]unicipalities/counties should also meaningfully include diverse stakeholders as part of their needs assessment and decision-making processes related to civilian oversight systems and other issues relevant to community/police relations."[34]

## Accountability through Police Chiefs and Elected Officials

Two law enforcement leaders raised concerns about citizen review boards at the N.C. City and County Managers Association Conference in February 2021.[35] Chief David Hess, Roxboro (North Carolina) Police Department and Chief Louis Dekmar, LaGrange (Georgia) Police Department have served in statewide and international leadership roles in local law enforcement. They stressed the value of partnerships and strong community relationships as the foundation for effective policing and for building two-way communication and trust.

---

32. "Citizen Advisory Boards," Pennsylvania Commission on Crime and Delinquency, accessed May 20, 2021, https://www.pccd.pa.gov/criminaljustice/Pages/Citizen-Advisory -Boards.aspx.

33. Ibid.

34. Ibid.

35. N.C. City and County Managers Association Conference, "Panel on the Future of Policing," Vimeo video, February 5, 2021, https://vimeo.com/504408559/cbdf04b4c3. Dekmar made small edits to the transcript of this video at the author's invitation.

Addressing a question about "whether citizen review boards can be an effective tool in building community confidence and what powers or involvement you think they might have," Hess and Dekmar expressed several reservations.[36]

Chief Hess noted how many North Carolina local law enforcement agencies have eleven sworn officers or fewer (about 100 communities) and explained that thus "town managers need to be aware that a one size fits all approach to citizen review boards may not be an appropriate choice for your local community."[37] Hess reported that the N.C. Association of Chiefs of Police "has long been concern[ed] about explicit bias of citizens toward officers in these smaller communities" and how this "could create inequitable outcomes on personnel actions."[38] Chief Hess sees other approaches as likely to be more "meaningful [. . .] to building community equity and dealing" with a range of community concerns about policing.[39]

Chief Dekmar, through his work with the International Association of Chiefs of Police, has not found any evidence that citizen review boards, on their own, increase police accountability. Dekmar explained that jurisdictions with police unions often have review boards, and there is an unhelpful dynamic of elected officials seeking police union support in elections, which undermines police accountability and prevents review boards from working appropriately.

Dekmar emphasized that the strongest, and most appropriate, forms of accountability lie with the elected officials responsible for a city's budget and overall public safety policies. He emphasized that these elected officials have the clearest responsibility for establishing police accountability. Dekmar lamented that some people see citizen review boards "as a panacea to address what really are political accountability issues that need to be addressed by elected officials."[40]

Dekmar places responsibility for officer conduct on the chief of police. He argued for providing the right types of tools to police leaders to pursue accountability, including "robust written directives, training consistent with those written directives, active supervision, the ability to engage effective accountability and discipline systems in order to take corrective action when officers behave or perform inconsistent with the agency standard, [and] ensuring that your police department is reviewing its practices through effective trend analysis."[41]

In turn, Dekmar highlighted the role of elected officials to actively seek information to judge police performance. He cited asking police leadership how an agency's use of force compares to the number of arrests, as well as how that data compares nationally. Tracking citizen complaints about officer conduct and

36. Ibid.
37. Ibid.
38. Ibid.
39. Ibid.
40. Ibid.
41. Ibid.

internal early warning systems are essential processes and components of policing for elected officials to understand.[42]

## Advice on CABs

On the 2016 International Association of Chiefs of Police (IACP) panel, Doug Wyllie[43] explained that "[u]nlike a Citizens Review Board, a Citizens Advisory Board is a group of people who meet on a regular basis to provide the chief of police with advice on a wide range of issues and exchange ideas."[44]

The panel consisted of two members of the Provo (Utah) Police Citizens Advisory Board (CAB) and the police chiefs of Provo and Salt Lake City. John King, Provo Chief of Police, said that the Provo CAB "is not a formal city organization, and therefore is not subject to the rules which can mire down public meetings," and the Provo CAB is "structured such that it is a relaxed environment which encourages dialog, not an hour of formal drudgery."[45] Salt Lake City Chief Mike Brown advised, "it's important to include people on the CAB who are your most ardent critics—the more diverse the group, the more perspectives will be brought to the table, and the better advice the chief will ultimately get."[46]

Guidance on operating a CAB included holding regular meetings, for which agendas should be made by citizens and the chief of police, as well as following the interests and concerns of the members of the CAB. The panel also gave a specific tip for law enforcement: "Bring to each meeting an idea about how to educate the public about law enforcement issues."[47]

Diversity of demographics and profession or work situation were cited as desirable aspects for a CAB to have. For orienting CAB members, attending a citizens police academy and (if eligible) participating in ride-alongs were recommended.

Drawing on the "Final Report of the President's Task Force on 21st Century Policing" (2015) Reece and Macy (2015) assert that "[e]ffective government is based on trust; thus, a central tenet of a citizen advisory board should be to build trust and two-way communication between the government (police) and the community."[48]

---

42. Ibid.

43. Doug Wyllie is a writer/columnist for *Police1* and a member of the International Law Enforcement Educators and Trainers Association (ILEETA). His profile can be found at https://www.police1.com/columnists/doug-wyllie/.

44. Doug Wyllie, "How to Successfully Create and Run a Citizens Advisory Board," *Police1*, October 16, 2016, https://www.police1.com/iacp-2016/articles/how-to-successfully-create-and-run-a-citizens-advisory-board-1YP7XhivFJ6PPCKa/.

45. Ibid.

46. Ibid.

47. Ibid.

48. John G. Reece and Judy Macy, "Citizen Advisory Boards in Contemporary Practice: A Practical Approach in Policing," *The Police Chief*, October, 2015, https://www.policechiefmagazine.org/citizen-advisory-boards-in-contemporary-practice-a-practical-approach-in-policing/?ref=7a04f5abf7ab746c4a68012838472330.

Reece and Macy (2015) add that, "Today, it is critically important for all police organizations to promote and cultivate citizen involvement with their agencies. However, implementing boards and commissions must be done thoughtfully and purposefully in order to establish a meaningful, effective relationship."[49] They call on police executives and elected officials to decide upon the amount of authority the board will have while remaining open to the importance of having citizen input and oversight.

Seeing a tension between police accountability and community trust and transparency, Reece and Macy (2015) also recommend that a CAB "should be limited in scope and purpose."[50] They caution against delegating too much power or authority to a CAB and argue that the head of a law enforcement agency "should retain some limited authority in the appointment of the board, accomplished through an established and transparent search process."[51]

A priority is "to establish a diversified board and to balance the interests and expertise found within the community as a whole," and CAB members "should clearly represent a constituency in order to be influential and supported by the population."[52] Reece and Macy (2015) advise that "the advisory board cannot be political. Each member must genuinely represent the community, or the fundamental objective of the board will be lost."[53] A 2019 IACP blog post suggested that a CAB should be between ten and twenty members, which would be "enough to represent your community, but not enough to stymie discussion."[54]

Reece and Macy (2015) also address two related considerations: term limits for CAB members and whether members should be approved by elected representatives. For a CAB to effectively address "the complex law enforcement incidents U.S. communities have experienced in the recent past," Reece and Macy (2015) recommend utilizing the "talents of the academic community" and seeking the "facilitation skills of an expert who can teach the advisory board about problem analysis and decision making."[55]

Moreover, a CAB should "mutually agree upon a consensus process in the development and approval of the recommendations. Transparency in the decision-making process will build trust among the participants."[56] Other advice includes addressing "potential conflicts among stakeholders early on," "mak[ing] sure that all participants are willing to work together to identify solutions," and ensuring

---

49. Ibid.
50. Ibid.
51. Ibid.
52. Ibid.
53. Ibid.
54. International Association of Chiefs of Police (IACP), "Promoting Community Involvement in Law Enforcement: Community Advisory Boards," *IACP Blog & News Releases,* May 6, 2019, https://www.theiacp.org/news/blog-post/promoting-community-involvement -in-law-enforcement-community-advisory-boards.
55. Reece and Macy, "Citizen Advisory Boards."
56. Ibid.

that the CAB "continues to play a meaningful role in the decision-making process."[57] The importance of being patient and allowing time for the CAB to gel is identified: "It can take time for the board to come together and achieve meaningful results."[58]

Reece and Macy (2015) conclude: "Citizen advisory boards are becoming important components of most law enforcement organizations and, when handled appropriately, will result in more democratic and effective organizations."[59]

---

57. IACP, "Promoting Community Involvement."
58. Ibid.
59. Reece and Macy, "Citizen Advisory Boards."

# Chapter 3

# Overview of Police Oversight Agencies Nationally and Recent Research on Effects of Civilian Oversight Agencies

## Quantity and Distribution of Police Oversight Agencies Nationally

Seeking a reliable count of civilian oversight agencies is difficult. There is no requirement for county or municipal law enforcement to inform a licensing, certification, or government body at the state or federal level of such bodies. Moreover, the committees and boards come in a range of powers and responsibilities such that what qualifies as "oversight" may be unclear.

According to the National Association for Civilian Oversight of Law Enforcement (NACOLE), there were "over 144 oversight bodies in the U.S." as of 2016.[1] NACOLE lists 143 agencies on its website, as of 2021.[2] However, in 2016 NACOLE leaders made a passing reference to "more than 200 oversight entities across the United States."[3]

The NACOLE 2021 website list covers thirty-seven states, and fifteen of the localities (cities or counties) list more than one oversight agency. While almost all the entries are for municipal or county jurisdictions, two are for university police (University of California, Davis and University of California, Berkeley) and one is a regional transit agency (San Francisco Bay Area Rapid Transit). Two are listed as joint city-county jurisdictions (Miami-Dade and Charlotte-Mecklenburg).

---

1. Joseph De Angelis, Richard Rosenthal, and Brian Buchner, *Civilian Oversight of Law Enforcement: A Review of the Strengths and Weaknesses of Various Models* (Tucson, AZ: National Association for Civilian Oversight of Law Enforcement, 2016), 5, https://d3n8a8pro7vhmx.cloudfront.net/nacole/pages/161/.

2. "Police Oversight by Jurisdiction (USA)," National Association for Civilian Oversight of Law Enforcement (NACOLE), accessed March 4, 2021, https://www.nacole.org/police_oversight_by_jurisdiction_usa. Confirming this count is problematic. Several entries have broken links to the listed entity (such as the links to the Ft. Lauderdale, FL; Inglewood, CA; and Baltimore, MD; entries). This list is in flux, according to NACOLE's statement on the "Police Oversight by Jurisdiction (USA)" webpage: "This list, which is for informational purposes only, represents agencies that came to the attention of NACOLE over time and also have websites. This IS NOT an exhaustive or complete list of oversight entities in the U.S. NACOLE continually adds to and revises the list."

3. Brian Buchner et al. (editors), *Guidebook for the Implementation of New or Revitalized Police Oversight* (Tucson, AZ: National Association for Civilian Oversight of Law Enforcement, 2016), 9.

The NACOLE 2021 list has entries for five North Carolina jurisdictions: Asheville, Charlotte-Mecklenburg, Durham, Greensboro, and Winston-Salem.[4] As presented below, several other North Carolina cities and one sheriff's department are identified as having either a review board or an advisory board: a count of at least sixteen CABs and CRBs.

The U.S. Department of Justice provides an estimate of the number of local law enforcements with CRBs or CABs. As part of regular data collection via national surveys conducted by the Bureau of Justice Statistics (BJS), a 2020 report presented 2016 data on the percent of local police departments with a civilian-complaint review board by size of population served. Across all the law enforcement agencies that responded, 11.3 percent reported having a civilian-complaint review board.[5]

For this 2016 data, BJS reports a pool of respondents that includes 2,135 local police departments and 600 sheriffs' offices.[6] Thus, an 11.3 percent positive response would result in slightly over three hundred civilian-complaint review boards. However, drawing on expert analysis of two of the North Carolina agencies that responded to the survey, the estimate of three hundred is probably too high.[7]

Finally, examining the location of CRBs, Ali and Pirog (2019) found that CRBs tend to be in cities with larger populations and above-average proportions of black residents (they drew from the NACOLE list and conducted an in-depth analysis of eighty jurisdictions with CRBs).[8] Ali and Pirog also reported that many of these bodies have been established since 2000.[9]

---

4. NACOLE, "Police Oversight by Jurisdiction (USA)."

5. Bureau of Justice Statistics, *Statistical Brief Local Police Departments: Policies and Procedures, 2016* (Washington, DC: U.S. Department of Justice, 2020), 7, https://www.bjs.gov/content/pub/pdf/lpdpp16.pdf.

6. "Data Collection: Law Enforcement Management and Administrative Statistics (LEMAS)," Bureau of Justice Statistics, accessed May 20, 2021, https://www.bjs.gov/index.cfm?ty=dcdetail&iid=248#Methodology. "A total of 2,779 agencies responded to the LEMAS questionnaire, for a response rate of 80%. The final database includes responses from 2,135 local police departments, 600 sheriffs' offices, and 49 state law enforcement agencies (including partial responses from 5 primary state police agencies). The overall response rate for local police departments was 82%, 74% for sheriffs' offices, and 90% for state law enforcement agencies."

7. Dr. James Brunet, email to the author, February 1, 2021.

8. Mir Usman Ali and Maureen Pirog, "Social Accountability and Institutional Change: The Case of Citizen Oversight of Police," *Public Administration Review* 79, no. 3 (2019): 411–26. Ali and Pirog present a map of the locations of the CRBs in their study. There are concentrations of CRBs on the West Coast, in the Maryland through Maine region, and clusters in Florida and Midwest states in the Minnesota-Missouri-Ohio region.

9. Ibid., 418.

## Research on the Effects of Civilian Oversight Agencies (COAs)

Oversight and accountability of U.S. law enforcement has a large research literature. However, twenty years ago, Samuel Walker, a leading researcher on police accountability, noted: "Although a number of oversight agencies have creditable records of success, there is a serious lack of research on the activities and effectiveness of oversight agencies. Many issues have not been investigated at all, while others have been investigated inadequately."[10] He highlighted several obstacles to "measuring the impact of any oversight activity on day-to-day policing."[11] In 2020, Walker and colleague Carol Archbold still find research lacking. After reviewing arguments about how civilian reviews of policing complaints should be more independent and objective, how such reviews can lead to better discipline and deter future misconduct, and how a more satisfactory complaint process can lead to higher citizen satisfaction with police officers in general, they say

> [t]here has been little scholarly research on citizen review of the police, however, and none of the assumptions outlined above have been investigated in studies that meet the highest standards of social science research. There are no studies, for example, that compare a civilian review agency with a police internal affairs unit. Nor are there any studies that investigate which form of civilian review is more effective than another and which factors contribute to success. As a result, it is not possible to make a judgment about whether civilian review of the police makes a positive contribution to police accountability.[12]

Walker identifies several factors for why trying to track the impact of citizen oversight on measures of police conduct and accountability is challenging. "Even in the best of circumstances citizen oversight is only one part of a mixed, multi-faceted system of accountability."[13] Walker describes internal and external influences on police accountability. The **internal influences** include formal policies and practices (ranging from recruitment and preservice training to discipline and rewards) and informal policing practices (i.e., on-the-job socialization and officer subculture). Regarding **external influences**, Walker denotes a tension between responsible political direction and improper political

---

10. Samuel Walker, *Police Accountability: The Role of Citizen Oversight* (Belmont, CA: Wadsworth/Thomson, 2001), 184.

11. Ibid., 184–85.

12. Walker and Archbold, *The New World*, 56. They do note that "citizen oversight of the police has, over the course of several decades, made some notable contributions to policy accountability while at the same time leaving many issues unaddressed. Most important, the movement for citizen oversight has established the principle that the police should be subject to external oversight."

13. Walker, *Police Accountability*, 185.

influence. He also identifies civic activism, the media, the courts, and citizen oversight as other external influences.[14]

For this book's purpose, a few recent studies regarding the effects of civilian oversight bodies on police accountability are most relevant. They focus on the three kinds of COAs and do not address CABs. The studies range from large quantitative analyses to comparisons of NACOLE standards in the five largest cities in Texas.

A common problem regarding civilian oversight is that it might inhibit police officers in their work due to concerns about how an external citizen body would assess a complaint or incident. Ali and Nicholson-Crotty (2020) studied citizen oversight agencies and their potential impact on policing of violent crime and homicides of police officers (HPOs). They conducted a statistical analysis and drew data from seventy-six cities with citizen oversight agencies (COAs).[15]

Ali and Nicholson-Crotty found that "while COAs with a narrow scope of authority can lead to an increase in the violent crime rate, COAs with a broad scope of authority lead to a decrease in the violent crime rate and a gradual reduction in HPOs. The implication is that it is not merely the existence of an accountability mechanism that can have an impact on performance; rather, it is the scope of authority of the mechanism that determines its impact."[16]

Another study examined the effects of COAs on institutional change. Ali and Pirog (2019) studied COAs in eighty jurisdictions (as of 2016) and created measures for each type of COA, based on the COAs' powers[17] (using the investigative, monitoring, and review/audit categories).[18] They investigated the possible effects of COAs on racial disparities in disorderly conduct arrests (DCAs) and police homicides of citizens (PHCs).

Their findings were that all three types of COAs reduced racial disparities in DCAs.[19] As for PHCs, they conclude that only investigative COAs had a positive impact in reducing the racial disparity in this type of police-community event. Ali and Pirog also examined if COA members appointed by "municipal district" had

---

14. Ibid., 186.

15. Mir Usman Ali and Sean Nicholson-Crotty, "Examining the Accountability-Performance Link: The Case of Citizen Oversight of Police," *Public Performance & Management Review* (2020), 15, https://doi.org/10.1080/15309576.2020.1806086. Out of 111 cities with COAs contacted for the study, 91 COAs in 88 cities responded. Researchers screened out 12 COAs for a net sample of 79 COAs from 76 cities.

16. Ibid., 22.

17. Ali and Pirog, "Social Accountability," 414–16.

18. Joseph De Angelis, Richard Rosenthal, and Brian Buchner, *Civilian Oversight of Law Enforcement: Assessing the Evidence* (National Association for Civilian Oversight of Law Enforcement, OJP Diagnostic Center, and U.S. Department of Justice, 2016), 22–32, https://d3n8a8pro7vhmx.cloudfront.net/nacole/pages/161/attachments/original/1481727974/NACOLE_AccessingtheEvidence_Final.pdf?1481727974.

19. Ali and Pirog, "Social Accountability," 421.

an impact on PHCs and DCAs. There was a statistically significant reduction in racial disparity for DCAs, but not for PHCs.[20]

Ali and Pirog also noted, given the distribution of COAs across the United States: "COAs tend to be established in large cities that have a relatively high proportion of blacks, and thus where interactions between blacks and police officers are likely to be more frequent."[21]

Holiday and Wagstaff (2021) compared cities with and without citizen review boards (CRBs), focusing on citizen attitudes about police accountability and fairness.[22] They collected data from community surveys conducted on behalf of local governments for residents' feedback on a wide range of government services. They applied this survey data to compare twenty-two cities with CRBs to twenty-six cities without CRBs.[23] Specifically, they "examine[d] the relationship between the presence of citizen oversight and citizens' satisfaction in the police, including their judgment that the police are procedurally just."[24]

Holiday and Wagstaff found a positive association between CRBs and the community's belief that the police are held accountable, treat people equally, and do a good job building community relationships. However, the authors caution that their dataset is "useful for exploratory research,"[25] but readers should not generalize the findings. Moreover, these results are associations, and the authors "do not assert a direct causal link between the presence of a CRB and measures of satisfaction and procedural justice, but merely show a general positive correlation exists between them."[26]

In a narrower, but more practice-oriented analysis, Sherman and Fulton (2020) studied the five largest Texas cities and determined how well those CRBs embodied NACOLE's list of thirteen principles for effective civilian oversight.[27]

---

20. Ibid., 422.

21. Ibid., 418.

22. Bradley S. Holliday and John H. Wagstaff, Jr., "The Relationship between Citizen Oversight and Procedural Justice Measures in Policing: An Exploratory Study," *American Journal of Criminal Justice* (2021), https://doi.org/10.1007/s12103-021-09610-3.

23. Ibid. The twenty-two cities had a "police department . . . overseen by a CRB, whether review-focused, investigator-focused, or advisory-focused and 26 surveys were from cities wherein the police have no form of [appointed] citizen oversight" (Holliday and Wagstaff, *Relationship*; no pagination in source). The surveyed cities range in population from 18,333 to 1,569,657, with a median population of 267,743, and three North Carolina cities are in their sample.

24. Ibid.

25. Ibid.

26. Ibid. Another important point is there is no claim that the citizens completing the general satisfaction survey about many kinds of municipal services "had any knowledge regarding the presence or absence of a CRB in their communities. Even if they knew their community had a CRB, we cannot be certain that knowledge directly resulted in higher measures of procedural justice apart from specifically asking respondents about the CRB" (Holliday and Wagstaff, *Relationship*; no pagination in source).

27. Sherman and Fulton, *Who's Policing the Police?*. Sherman and Fulton's study was prompted by a Fall 2020 task force, on which Fulton served, that examined how to improve the Houston CRB.

The value of this study is the direct comparison of five oversight agencies, three of which were less than two years old. A possible shortcoming for North Carolina public officials is that all five cities are very large and thus quite different from most North Carolina cities.

Using the thirteen NACOLE principles, Sherman and Fulton "examined each city's oversight board to see how well they aligned (or diverged) from best practices."[28] Their recommendations emphasize placing civilian oversight within "a larger police accountability project" that includes "making . . . data more publicly available (and not only crime data, but institutional and complaint data as well)," improving police-resident communication, and aligning different oversight institutions.[29] Sherman and Fulton also note that Texas state law may create barriers to citizen oversight and recommend assuring sufficient powers and staffing for oversight to work, including a "strong legal basis" for oversight agencies and training for board members. They note that oversight is usually a part of the collective bargaining agreement.[30]

None of these studies appear to examine citizen advisory boards on law enforcement or public safety, which exist in several North Carolina cities.

---

28. Ibid., 2.
29. Ibid., 18.
30. Ibid., 18–20.

# Chapter 4

# Comparison of North Carolina Cities and Counties with Civilian Advisory or Review Boards

## Introduction

This chapter presents information about and compares and contrasts localities with citizen advisory boards (CABs) or citizen review boards (CRBs). The following sections provide a snapshot of North Carolina's CABs and CRBs to educate North Carolina law enforcement, local government leaders, and interested citizens of the functions and structures of these boards.

Accompanying the general comparisons are brief profiles of selected CABs and CRBs in "Appendix A. Profiles of Civilian Advisory (CABs) and Review Boards (CRBs) in North Carolina." The profiles will assist readers attempting to locate communities and forms of CABs and CRBs relevant to their interests.[1]

## Location, Population, and Jurisdictions of Civilian Advisory (CABs) and Review Boards (CRBs) in North Carolina

Sixteen cities and three sheriffs' offices in North Carolina with civilian advisory (CABs) and review boards (CRBs) were located through websites and publications and an inquiry to members of the N.C. Association of Chiefs of Police. Three other cities in North Carolina are considering establishment of or actively engaging in the development of a CAB or CRB (Fayetteville, Hillsborough, and Wilmington).

CABs and CRBs are most common in North Carolina's larger cities. The five largest cities have a CAB or CRB (Charlotte, Durham, Greensboro, Raleigh,

---

1. The civilian advisory (CABs) and review boards (CRBs) in North Carolina have their own unique names. For example, the official name of the citizen advisory board in Chapel Hill is the "Chapel Hill Community Policing Advisory Committee (CPAC)." In this book, each CAB or CRB is referred to by its official name, as in the "Chapel Hill Policing Advisory Committee (CPAC)," or, in a more generic sense, as in "Chapel Hill's citizen advisory board (CAB)," interchangeably.

and Winston-Salem), and nine of the fifteen largest cities have a CAB or CRB (including Asheville, Chapel Hill, Greenville, and Wilmington).[2]

The Durham County Sheriff's Office established a CAB in 2019, and the Guilford County Sheriff's Office created a CAB (named as a "community roundtable") in 2020. Guilford has the third largest population of North Carolina counties, and Durham has the sixth largest.[3]

Six medium to smaller cities have a CAB. Medium-sized cities include Burlington (with a population of about 53,500) and Salisbury (with a population of about 34,000).[4] Joining the larger cities of Durham and Raleigh is a cluster of communities with CABs in the Research Triangle area, including Benson, Chapel Hill, Knightdale, and Morrisville (with Hillsborough currently developing a CAB). There is no indication of influence, coordination, or cross-fertilization of CABs in this region. The formation of Salisbury's CAB in 2018 influenced the nearby town of Spencer (with a population of about 3,300) to form its own CAB in 2020.[5]

## When the CABs and CRBs Were Created

The first CAB established in North Carolina was in New Bern, in the form of the New Bern Police Civil Service Board (PCSB), in the 1950s. The PCSB was unusual in its specific advisory role in the recruitment and hiring of officers. Its advisory function ended in 2016, although the PCSB continues to hear officers' appeals of certain disciplinary actions or termination of employment. Thus, the PCSB does not presently fit the definition of a CAB definition (see Appendix A for more information about the PCSB).

Five jurisdictions formed CABs and CRBs from 1991 to 2001. Between 1998 and 2003, four large cities received North Carolina General Assembly local legislation to provide access to protected public documents (such as personnel information) for their CRBs to operate. New Bern established the first CRB in the state, followed by the larger cities of Winston-Salem (1993), Charlotte/Mecklenburg (1996), Durham (1998), and Greensboro (2001). No other CRBs have been created since 2001.

---

2. Fayetteville, the sixth largest city in North Carolina, currently has a CRB in development. "North Carolina Cities by Population," North Carolina Demographics by Cubit, accessed May 19, 2021, https://www.northcarolina-demographics.com/cities_by_population.

3. "North Carolina Cities by Population," North Carolina Demographics by Cubit, accessed May 19, 2021, https://www.northcarolina-demographics.com/counties_by_population.

4. Ibid.

5. Mike T. James (Spencer Police Chief), email message to author, April 30, 2021.

## Table 1. North Carolina CABs and CRBs: Date Created, Location, and Type of Board

| Date established | City or county | Type of board | Number of members |
|---|---|---|---|
| 1950s[a] | New Bern | Review (officer hiring only until 2016) | 5 |
| 1991 | Asheville | Advisory | 9 |
| 1993 | Winston-Salem | Review | 11 |
| 1996 | Charlotte/Mecklenburg | Review | 11 |
|  | Greenville | Advisory | 7 |
| 1998 | City of Durham | Review | 9 |
| 2001 | Greensboro—Police Community Review Board (PCRB) | Review | 7 |
|  | Greensboro—Greensboro Criminal Justice Advisory Commission (GCJAC) | Advisory | 9 |
| 2009 | Benson | Advisory | 6 |
| 2011 | Chapel Hill | Advisory | 9 |
| 2013 | Morrisville | Advisory | 11 |
| 2018 | Knightdale (revised 2020; originally "police only," then late 2018 or early 2019, it became "police and fire," and then back to police only in 2020) | Advisory | 5 |
|  | Salisbury | Advisory | 25 |
| 2019 | Durham County Sheriff | Advisory | 25 |
| 2020 | Burlington | Advisory | 15–20 |
|  | Guilford County Sheriff | Advisory | 32 |
|  | Raleigh | Advisory | 9 |
| 2021 | Alamance County Sheriff | Advisory | 6 |
|  | Manteo | Advisory | 6 |
|  | Spencer | Advisory | 7–9 |

a. No longer considered a civilian advisory board (CAB), per the definition established in this book, as of 2016.

## North Carolina CRBs

Four cities in North Carolina have boards designed to hear appeals from people who allege that the police have mistreated them. If the aggrieved citizens are unsatisfied with the police department's actions on their complaint, they may proceed to a CRB. All four CRBs are in major cities: Charlotte, Durham, Greensboro, and Winston-Salem (see Appendix A for more details about these cities' CRBs).

All these bodies that provide civilian oversight of complaints about police conduct fit the National Association for Civilian Oversight of Law Enforcement's (NACOLE) **review-focused model**. This model guides boards through the reassessment of completed investigations by reviewing the quality of police internal affairs investigations. Each appeal must be initiated by the complainant who is not satisfied with the determination of the internal affairs (or professional standards) investigation and outcome. Each CRB determines the necessity of a hearing in response to a complaint (see the "Three Models of Oversight" section in Chapter 1 for a full description of NACOLE's review-focused model).

As shown in the profiles of the CRBs of Charlotte, Durham, Greensboro, and Winston-Salem (see Appendix A), the work of North Carolina CRBs is formal and quasi-judicial, with explicit procedures on what complainants must provide to initiate an appeal. In addressing appeals, these CRBs aim to determine whether police departments properly investigated (by following department procedures) and did not abuse discretion in considering the complaints. However, none of the four CRBs have the final say on an appeal. The Durham Civilian Police Review Board (CPRB) makes a recommendation to the city manager, who can either sustain or reject the outcome of the police department's investigation. The same procedure is used by the Greensboro Police Community Review Board (PCRB), although the PCRB can comment on the action of the city manager (see the Greensboro Criminal Justice Advisory Commission (GCJAC) and Police Community Review Board (PCRB) profile in Appendix A for more detail). The Charlotte Citizens Review Board (CCRB) sends a summary of facts to the chief of police and the city manager. The Winston-Salem Citizens' Police Review Board (CPRB) sends summary reports to the Winston-Salem Public Safety Committee and the city manager.

For these four CRBs, the number of appeals that proceed to a hearing is small: usually one to three appeals per year. Among the four CRBs discussed here, the Charlotte CRB heard the most appeals during the 2016–2017 session: a total of five appeals.

Finally, North Carolina CRBs have varying levels of participation in public outreach and education. The GCJAC's scope of work goes beyond addressing complaints against police, as the commission can address court system issues. In recent years, the Durham City Council added a public outreach obligation to the Durham CPRB's work. Charlotte and Winston-Salem do not require community outreach or education work from their CRB members.

## North Carolina CABs

Civilian advisory boards (CABs) are the majority of formally appointed civilian bodies in North Carolina: twelve cities and three counties operate CABs. The CABs are fairly similar to each other; they all serve as a standing forum for voices from the community and for receiving and discussing information from the police or sheriff's department. The most common, overarching goal of these CABs is promoting strong relations between the community and law enforcement. Specific goals of CABs vary, but the themes are

- community voice,
- awareness and education,
- support of law enforcement,
- input on law enforcement functions and community concerns, and
- specific topics for attention and comment.

The following sections elaborate on these themes of North Carolina CABs; the subsequent sections describe the appointment of members to CRBs and CABs, as well as the steps taken by these boards to represent the demographics of the community.

### Community Voice

A CAB's goal of representing the community can be implicit or explicit. For Benson's CAB, the Benson Police Advisory Commission (PAC), the goal of community representation is explicit. According to its website, the Benson PAC aims to "[r]epresent the point of view of the citizens of Benson" and "to review and provide a community perspective and recommendations concerning [law enforcement] programs and procedures."[6] For more information on the Benson Police Advisory Commission, see Appendix A.

Sometimes, a CAB is established with the intention of focusing on particular parts of the community. For example, the charter that established the Salisbury Police Department Police Chief's Citizen Advisory Board (CAB) prioritizes the fostering of communication with marginalized groups.[7] For more information on the Salisbury CAB, see Appendix A. Spencer's CAB, the Spencer Chief's Citizen Advisory Board, seeks to act as "a means of enhancing police/community relations, communications, transparency, community confidence and trust."[8] For more information on Spencer's CAB, see Appendix A.

In Greenville, the police department depends on the Police Community Relations Committee (PCRC) to solicit feedback from the public and organize community outreach opportunities (see Appendix A for more information about the Greenville PCRC). Similarly, the Raleigh Police Advisory Board (PAB) has

---

6. "Police Advisory Commission," Town of Benson, accessed February 22, 2021, https://www.townofbenson.com/2169/Police-Advisory-Commission.

7. *Charter of the Salisbury Police Department Police Chief's Citizen Advisory Board* (2018), 3.

8. *Spencer Police Department Police Chief's Citizen Advisory Board Charter*, Article IV.

a broad mandate for "[e]ngaging community members through educational outreach on Raleigh Police Department directives."[9] See Appendix A for more information about the Raleigh PAB.

Some CABs help to organize outreach events for hearing community concerns. For instance, the Asheville Citizens Police Advisory Committee (CPAC) facilitates town hall meetings (for more information about the Asheville CPAC, see Appendix A), and the Chapel Hill Community Policing Advisory Committee (CPAC) convened an August 2020 community listening session in the wake of the summer 2020 protests in Chapel Hill and many other cities (for more information about the Chapel Hill CPAC, see Appendix A).

## Awareness and Education

The second common function for CABs is to be part of law enforcement outreach to the community by providing information about policing. Examples include the following:

- Benson's CAB promotes public awareness of the town's police services and programs.[10]
- Asheville's CAB holds community engagement events that educate the public on how to file complaints.[11]
- The Guilford County Sheriff's Community Roundtable typically begins with a presentation about a function of the sheriff's office, with the goal of the roundtable members providing accurate information to their community contacts. For more information on Guilford's Community Roundtable, see Appendix A.

The Greenville Police Department works with the Greenville Police Community Relations Committee (see Appendix A) to solicit feedback from the public and organize community outreach opportunities. Topics for community events have included neighborhood policing and post-arrest rehabilitation.[12]

The types of topics and depth of information vary among CABs. Information on crime statistics and general policing strategies are common points of discussion. On the other hand, the Benson CAB members are informed of general personnel information (e.g., open positions, hiring status, and promotions).

Overall, law enforcement leaders aim to educate CABs about policing resources and strategies, and to gain their assistance for informing segments of the wider

---

9. "Police Advisory Board," Raleigh, accessed February 18, 2021, https://raleighnc.gov/police-advisory-board.

10. Town of Benson, "Police Advisory Commission."

11. For example, the event plans detailed in the Asheville Citizens Police Advisory Committee's (CPAC) meeting agenda for March 4, 2020, which can be found at https://drive.google.com/file/d/1yAYmioXFrhBW4Oi0K833LsTIDbDyNiFl/view.

12. Greenville Police Community Relations Committee (PCRC), *Summary Minutes for the Police Community Relations Committee* (May 14, 2019), https://www.greenvillenc.gov/home/showdocument?id=18731.

community of the challenges and approaches to public safety. The activities to increase information and awareness are closely related to the next theme of CABs.

## Support of Law Enforcement

The heightened interaction between CAB members and law enforcement leaders can contribute to community support of law enforcement. Sometimes the goal is presented in CAB documents as *building the support of law enforcement* and other times as *improving two-way relations* between law enforcement and the community.

One illustration is the Spencer CAB's goal to support "a close relationship between the Spencer Police Department and the community," and to be "a means of enhancing police/community relations, communications, transparency, community confidence and trust."[13] One of the Chapel Hill CPAC's goals is to "[s]erve as a liaison to enhance community and police relations."[14] In February 2020, Greenville's PCRC welcomed East Carolina University students to a roundtable with the Greenville Police Department about the police department's relationship with college students. Each party had the opportunity to air its grievances and set expectations for future interactions.[15]

## Input on Law Enforcement Functions and Community Concerns

Many CABs are charged with providing input on police department policies and public engagement initiatives. Chapel Hill's CAB must "[m]ake recommendations to the Town Manager and Chief of Police regarding organizational matters and procedures."[16] Another example is the Raleigh CAB's charge to review existing police department procedures and contribute to fair policy development.[17]

Other CABs, by ordinance, charter, or practice, have targeted tasks. For example, the Chapel Hill CPAC and the Knightdale Community Policing Advisory Board (CPAB) (see Appendix A for more information about the Knightdale CPAB) review and advise on the curriculum of their respective municipality's citizen police academy. Another task among some citizen advisory boards is participation in obtaining a Commission on Accreditation for Law Enforcement Agencies (CALEA) certification. For example, the Burlington

---

13. *Spencer Police Department Police Chief's Citizen Advisory Board Charter,* Article IV.

14. Chapel Hill Town Council, *A Resolution to Establish a Community Policing Advisory Committee for the Town of Chapel Hill (2011-03-28/R-9)* (March 28, 2011), http://chapelhill.granicus.com/MetaViewer.php?view_id=&clip_id=975&meta_id=114560.

15. Greenville PCRC, *Summary Minutes for the Police Community Relations Committee,* February 11, 2020. A Word document of these meeting minutes can be found here: https://www.greenvillenc.gov/government/city-council/boards-and-commissions/police-community-relations-committee/2020-police-community-relations-committee-meeting-schedule-and-agendas.

16. Chapel Hill Town Council, *A Resolution to Establish a Community Policing Advisory Committee.*

17. "Police Advisory Board," Raleigh, accessed May 18, 2021, https://raleighnc.gov/police-advisory-board.

Community Police Advisory Team (CPAT) "is an important part of maintaining Burlington's Commission on Accreditation for Law Enforcement Agencies (CALEA) status. Burlington has held this accreditation in good standing for 27 years. CPAT will assist in components of accreditation through the review of annual reports on use of force, traffic stops, pursuits, and community relations metrics."[18] For more information on the Burlington CPAT, see Appendix A.

## Specific Topics for Attention and Comment

The issues and topics considered by CABs often arise from the questions and concerns posed by the CAB members themselves. The range of issues, degrees of input, and outcomes vary considerably. Details can be found in Appendix A, but Table 2 provides a summary.

## Table 2. Sample of Topics and Concerns of North Carolina CABs

| CAB | Topics or concerns addressed |
| --- | --- |
| Benson Police Advisory Commission (PAC) | • Community watch<br>• Speed limit enforcement<br>• Opioids and overdoses<br>• Animal control |
| Chapel Hill Community Policing Advisory Committee (CPAC) | • Data analytics on various public safety issues affecting equitable policing |
| Charlotte Citizens' Review Board (CCRB)[a] | • Use of force on resistant subjects<br>• Increasing accessibility to the appeals process |
| Greensboro Criminal Justice Advisory Commission (GCJAC) | • Dealing with people in an extremely agitated state<br>• Distinguishing between hemp and marijuana and advice that marijuana violations be deprioritized<br>• Voluntary consent-to-search policy |
| Greenville Police Community Relations Committee (PCRC) | • Reducing recidivism of repeat offenders<br>• Neighborhood policing |
| Knightdale Community Police Advisory Board (CPAB) | • False alarm ordinance<br>• Human trafficking |
| Morrisville's Public Safety Advisory Committee (PSAC) | • Traffic ticket appeals<br>• Pedestrian and bicycle safety<br>• Use of tasers<br>• Car break-ins |
| Winston-Salem Citizens' Police Review Board (CPRB)[b] | • Body cameras and the storage of video footage |

a. Although the Charlotte CRB is technically a review board, it is included here because it has some CAB functions.
b. As with the Charlotte CRB, the Winston-Salem CPRB is a review board, but it is included here because it has some CAB functions.

18. Burlington Police Department, *Community Police Advisory Team Formation and Charter* (November 2020), 2, https://www.burlingtonnc.gov/DocumentCenter/View/19109/BPD-CPAT-Charter-Revised-042221?bidId=.

Morrisville's Public Safety Advisory Committee (PSAC) makes recommendations for the traffic ticket appeals process (which is a unique responsibility among all CABs in North Carolina) and has set a goal to prioritize pedestrian and bicycle safety initiatives. Current topics for meetings include car break-ins and the use of tasers in police interactions (see Appendix A for more about the Morrisville Public Safety Advisory Committee (PSAC)).

The Charlotte Citizens' Review Board (CRB) has made recommendations regarding the use of force on resistant subjects (although the Charlotte CRB is technically a review board, it is included in this section because it has some CAB functions). The board has also addressed increasing accessibility to the appeals process through regular updates of the Charlotte CRB website. How to decrease recidivism among repeat offenders was a concern of the Greenville Police Community Relations Committee (PCRC).

Some members of the Chapel Hill Community Policing Advisory Committee (CPAC) are focusing on data analytics for various issues on public safety and equitable policing. The Knightdale Community Policing Advisory Board (CPAB) has made public safety presentations to the city council on revisions to the false alarm ordinance, and aims to learn more about human trafficking and policing strategies.

With the combination of a long-standing CAB, the Greensboro Criminal Justice Advisory Commission (GCJAC), and a subcommittee to review individual complaints, the Greensboro Police Community Review Board (PCRB), Greensboro has addressed an interesting range of topics:

- At the request of the Greensboro City Council, the GCJAC reviewed the police department's voluntary consent-to-search policy.
- The GCJAC has addressed concerns about law enforcement distinguishing between hemp and marijuana. The commission's recommendation was that "[a]s marijuana and hemp are indistinguishable from each other by field tests, the presence of the odor of hemp or marijuana should not be used as a reason for probable cause to search." The GCJAC added that marijuana violations should be deprioritized.[19]
- In 2019, the Restraint Review Subcommittee of the GCJAC met with the Greensboro Police Department's Restraint Review Committee to address procedures and devices to be used when dealing with individuals that are in an extremely agitated state.

## CRBs and CABs: Preparation and Expectations of Members

CRB members, due to the quasi-judicial nature of their work, have extensive training in police investigation principles and techniques, as well as other

---

19. Recommendation from the Greensboro Criminal Justice Advisory Commission (GCJAC) on hemp versus marijuana (on file with author).

parts of the criminal justice system. For example, the Durham Civilian Police Review Board (CPRB) has a training program for members that covers eleven topics delivered by staff from the Durham City Manager's Office, Durham City Attorney's Office, and Durham Police Department. All CRBs in North Carolina require that members complete training before they can participate in a hearing.

For CAB and CRB members, participation in ride-alongs to observe and better understand frontline officers is a common expectation (e.g., the Benson Police Advisory Commission (PAC), and the Durham CPRB). Some boards require that members obtain a certain number of hours in a ride-along per quarter or year, while other boards simply encourage member participation in ride-alongs.

Another common qualification for membership in a CRB or CAB in North Carolina is attendance in the respective municipality's citizen police academy, if such an education program is offered by the jurisdiction (e.g., such as the citizen police academy offered in Durham, which members of the Durham County Sheriff's Community Advisory Board (CAB) attend (for more details about the Durham County Sheriff's CAB, see Appendix A). The Asheville CPAC asks members to attend the city's citizens' police academy after appointment. The Charlotte Citizens' Review Board (CRB) requires members to attend the city's police citizens' academy, and members must also receive training on relevant legal, policy, and cultural awareness issues, as required by the city manager, before they can participate in board activities. Moreover, Charlotte CRB members must complete eight hours of continuing education training each year.

Four CABs (Greenville, Knightdale, Salisbury, and Spencer) include a code of ethics or code of conduct for members. The Salisbury Code of Ethics addresses personal integrity; independent and thorough oversight; transparency and confidentiality; respectful and unbiassed treatment; outreach and relationships with stakeholders; agency self-examination and commitment to policy review; and professional excellence.[20] Spencer's Code of Ethics is substantially the same.[21] In Greenville, members must commit to acting in a nonpartisan fashion, regularly updating the council member who appointed them of their contributions, and actively pursuing feedback from citizens.[22] The Knightdale CAB's Code of Ethics applies to all appointed advisory boards in its jurisdiction.[23]

Burlington is unique in setting a professional membership standard not for the CAB members, but for the city manager and chief of police. The Burlington CPAT charter requires that "the City Manager and Chief of Police must

---

20. *Charter of the Salisbury Police Department Police Chief's Citizen Advisory Board* (2018), 2.

21. Jerry Stokes (Salisbury Police Chief), email message to author, March 23, 2021.

22. Greenville PCRC, *Code of Conduct*, 4.

23. Knightdale, *Code of Ethics for Citizen Advisory Board Members of the Town of Knightdale, North Carolina*, https://www.knightdalenc.gov/sites/default/files/uploads/nb_-_code_of_ethics_for_boards_and_committees_-_updated_draft.pdf.

maintain membership in the National Association of Civilian Oversight for Law Enforcement (NACOLE) on behalf of the City."[24]

### Reports and Internal Organization

A few advisory committees provide formal reports to the city council or general community. For example, the Chapel Hill Community Policing Advisory Committee (CPAC) is to "[p]rovide an annual report to Council on a Council requested topic."[25]

Finally, there are two instances of CABs considering or creating subcommittees. For example, in fall 2020 the Chapel Hill CPAC formed several subcommittees, including community outreach, community safety implementation, and community safety data acquisition and analysis.[26] As of late 2020, the Morrisville Public Safety Advisory Committee is considering establishing a subcommittee on police reform.[27]

### Member Selection or Appointment

Appointments are made either by the city council or by an individual person. Table 3 summarizes the ways CAB and CRB members are appointed.

One method is selection by the chief law enforcement official. This method applies to the Alamance County Citizens' Public Safety Advisory Board, Durham County Sheriff's CAB, Guilford County Sheriff's Community Roundtable, Salisbury CAB, and Spencer CAB. A second method is the city council making appointments, but this practice varies among boards. In some cases, applicants or nominees are considered by the council with little or no prior steps for selection. However, some municipalities have designations for individual council members and/or the mayor to take the first step toward choosing a particular person. As described below, some municipalities have mixed systems of appointments.

In Charlotte, eleven members serve on the CRB. Three members are appointed by the mayor, five members are appointed by the city council, and three members are appointed by the city manager. In Greenville, the PCRC consists of seven members appointed by the city council. Five of those individuals are tapped by the council representative of one of the five districts of the city. Each district council member chooses a PCRC member. The council member at-large and the mayor each select a member. All nominees are seated by a vote of the entire city council.

24. Burlington Police Department, *Community Police Advisory Team Formation and Charter* (last revised January 26, 2021; adopted by City Council on February 2, 2021; adopted by City Council May 4, 2021), https://www.burlingtonnc.gov/DocumentCenter/View/19109 /BPD-CPAT-Charter-Revised-042221?bidId=.

25. Chapel Hill Town Council, *A Resolution to Establish a Community Policing Advisory Committee.*

26. Joshua Romero (CPAC Co-Chair), email correspondence with author, February 22, 2021.

27. Bill Granger (Morrisville Fire Department), in discussion with author, February 23, 2021.

The Durham City Manager appoints Durham CRB members, and the Durham City Council reviews those appointments before they are finalized. Finally, one member of the Benson Board of Commissioners serves on the Benson CAB as a member.

## Table 3. Summary of the Ways CAB and CRB Members Are Appointed

| How members are appointed | Boards |
| --- | --- |
| Law enforcement leader selects | Alamance County Citizens' Public Safety Advisory Board (PSAB) ; Alamance County Sheriff selects |
| | Durham County Sheriff's Community Advisory Board (CAB); Durham County Sheriff selects |
| | Guilford County Sheriff's Community Roundtable; Guilford County Sheriff selects |
| | Salisbury Police Chief's Citizen Advisory Board (CAB); Salisbury Chief of Police selects |
| | Spencer Chief's Citizen Advisory Board (CAB); Spencer Chief of Police selects |
| Individual "first-step" appointment power | Greenville Police Community Relations Committee (PCRC); Mayor, council member at-large, and five district council members nominate, chosen by vote of full council. |
| City manager selects, with city council review | Durham Civilian Police Review Board (CPRB) |
| City council selects | Benson Police Advisory Commission (PAC) |
| | Burlington Community Police Advisory Team (CPAT) |
| | Chapel Hill Community Policing Advisory Committee (CPAC) |
| | Knightdale Community Policing Advisory Board (CPAB) |
| | Manteo Community-Police Advisory Board[a] |
| | Morrisville Public Safety Advisory Committee (PSAC) |
| | Winston-Salem Citizens' Police Review Board (CPRB) |
| City council selects; seats are designated to certain groups | Raleigh Police Advisory Board (PAB); The Raleigh PAB has nine seats, four of which are designated to a mental health provider, victim advocate, attorney, and member of the LGBT community. |
| | Asheville Citizens/Police Advisory Committee (CPAC); The Asheville CPAC should have at least one member who is a public housing resident and one member who is a public housing authority staff member. |
| Separate paths to appointment | Charlotte Citizens' Review Board (CCRB)<br>1. Mayor appoints three members;<br>2. city manager appoints three members; and<br>3. city council appoints five members. |
| | Greensboro Police Community Review Board (PCRB)<br>1. Four selected from members of the Greensboro Criminal Justice Advisory Commission (GCJAC); and<br>2. three appointed by the mayor, with city council concurrence. |

a. For more information about the Manteo Community-Police Advisory Board, see Appendix A.

## Diversity and Community Representation

A stated goal for most CABs and CRBs is for their membership to represent the community. Some specifically address diversity of the community's demographics and other group or individual identity factors. How those interests in broad representation or diversity are addressed by CABs and CRBs has interesting variations.

Most CABs' and CRBs' mission statements or other documents state the goal of representation or diversity without detailed guidance. However, some CABs and CRBs, which are described in the following sections, specify factors that contribute to such representation.

### Geographic Location

One specific factor for ensuring diversity of representation is geographic location. The Greenville PCRC consists of seven members appointed by the Greenville City Council. Five of those individuals each represent one of the five districts of the city.

Like Greenville, the Burlington CPAT seeks "[s]everal geographic based community members, striving to include at least one member from each of the City's four geographic police patrol zones."[28] Asheville also strives for geographic diversity on its CAB. Five members of the Asheville CPAC represent the north, south, east, west, and central parts of the city.

### Public Information: Gender and Race/Ethnicity of Members

Winston-Salem's Citizens' Police Review Board identifies members by categories of race, ethnicity, and gender.[29] For current members, the designations are black male, black female, Asian male, white male, and white female (see the sidebar on the next page).

---

28. *Burlington Community Police Advisory Team Charter* (November 13, 2020), 4, https://www.burlingtonnc.gov/DocumentCenter/View/19109/BPD-CPAT-Charter-Revised-042221?bidId=.

29. This information can be found on the Winston-Salem Citizens' Police Review Board's (CPRB) website: https://www.cityofws.org/849/Citizens-Police-Review-Board.

## Current Membership of the Winston-Salem Citizens' Police Review Board (CPRB)

| Name | Asian | Race Black | White | Gender Female | Male | Term | Expiration |
|---|---|---|---|---|---|---|---|
| Tony Burton, Chairman | | ● | | | ● | 2 | April 2023 |
| Michael Rieker, Vice Chair | | | ● | | ● | 1 | April 2021 |
| Brittany Speas | | ● | | ● | | 1 | April 2022 |
| Theodis Chunn | | ● | | | ● | 2 | April 2024 |
| Pamela Corbett | | | ● | | | 2 | April 2023 |
| Beverly Carter-Levy | | ● | | ● | | 2 | April 2022 |
| Twana Wellman Roebuck | | ● | | ● | | 2 | April 2022 |
| Emer James Masicampo | ● | | | | ● | 1 | April 2022 |
| Kathy McLean | | | ● | ● | | 2 | April 2023 |
| Leon McCullough | | ● | | | ● | 2 | April 2023 |
| Michael S. Fradin | | | ● | | ● | 1 | April 2022 |
| Jaquae Perkins | | ● | | ● | | 1 | April 2024 |

*Source:* Adapted from "Citizens' Police Review Board," Winston-Salem, North Carolina, last accessed July 13, 2021, https://www.cityofws.org/849/Citizens-Police-Review-Board.

*By Profession and Community Connection*

Raleigh's Police Advisory Board (PAB) designates four member "slots" by expertise or community connection:

- mental health provider,
- victim advocate,
- attorney, and
- a member of the LGBT community.[30]

There are nine members in total on the Raleigh PAB.

Burlington's, Salisbury's, and Spencer's CABs reference the goal of having at least one NAACP representative on their respective boards. In addition to aiming for geographic representation, the Salisbury Police Chief's CAB seeks one

---

30. Raleigh City Council Meeting, *Regular Meeting-Third Tuesday-Afternoon Session* (June 16, 2020), https://go.boarddocs.com/nc/raleigh/Board.nsf/goto?open&id=AMXHS2497127.

representative from each of the major institutions in the city, such as Livingstone College and Catawba College.[1]

The Asheville CPAC is unique in designating two member slots related to public housing. One seat is for a resident of public housing, and another is for a staff member of the housing authority.

The Burlington CPAT has the most extensive list of desired varieties of identities for membership as a whole. The Burlington CPAT charter states: "City Council will strive (flexibility may be needed) to identify and select members from the categories as follows,"[2] referring to a thirteen-item list with a wide range of categories, including:

- work or professional role ("one line level police employee," and the K-12 and community college systems);
- racial group, ethnic group, or sexual orientation (e.g., African American community, Hispanic/Latinx community, LGBTQ community);
- youth;
- members of the local chapter of the National Alliance on Mental Illness;
- representatives from "community of justice-involved persons"; and
- "[a]ll [f]aith communities, including ministerial/clergy associations, the Muslim faith community, the Christian faith community, and all other faith communities in Burlington."[3]

## Conclusion

This book has presented an overview of police accountability through appointed civilian bodies and described the North Carolina city- and county-level instances of citizen advisory (CABs) and review boards (CRBs). Chapter 1 examined the reasons to consider CABS and CRBs, discussed the goals and functions of such appointed civilian bodies, and described the three models of oversight, as well as a fourth model, which is an advisory role. Experience in the United States from several sources provided guidance on forming and managing CABs and CRBs. Chapter 2 discussed the motivating factors, formation, and management of CABs and CRBs. Chapter 3 described the quantity and distribution of police oversight agencies nationally, and paid particular attention to some of the most recent research and field evaluations of the effects of civilian oversight agencies (COA) and CRBs on police accountability.

Chapter 4 presented the picture of civilian bodies concerning police accountability in North Carolina by comparing sixteen municipal CABs/CRBs and three sheriffs' offices with a CAB. The chapter described when these

---

1. Jerry Stokes (Salisbury Police Chief), email message to author, March 23, 2021.
2. *Burlington Community Police Advisory Team Charter* (November 13, 2020), 3.
3. Ibid.

appointed civilian bodies were established, their duties, and their membership and methods of appointment. Some of the topics addressed by CABs offer a snapshot of the CAB and CRB landscape in North Carolina.

With three other cities in North Carolina currently exploring or actively developing a CAB or CRB, this book serves as a snapshot of basic information for future examination of CABs' and CRBs' functions, as well as a foundation for assessment of CABs' and CRBs' impact on police accountability and community involvement.

# Appendix A

# Profiles of Civilian Advisory (CABs) and Review Boards (CRBs) in North Carolina

*Note*: The number of cities in North Carolina with advisory or review boards is likely to increase. As of June 9, 2021, three cities are in the process of establishing or are considering such bodies: Fayetteville, Hillsborough, and Wilmington.

## The Alamance County Citizens' Public Safety Advisory Board (ACCPSAB)

In Summer 2020, in reaction to the death of George Floyd, community leaders called for the establishment of a law enforcement review board that would represent all of Alamance County. The proposal was for a single civilian body covering municipal police forces and the county sheriff. In Fall 2020, Sheriff Terry S. Johnson judged that such a multi-jurisdiction effort was unlikely to form quickly, so he responded by creating an advisory board for the sheriff's office.

The Alamance County Citizens' Public Safety Advisory Board (ACCPSAB) was established in early 2021 and had its first meeting in February 2021. The board's mission is to "address public safety and related concerns in particular law enforcement and community relation concerns in order to promote a better quality of life for all citizens in Alamance County."[1] The board's vision is to "provide the citizens of Alamance County with an objective body to promote an open avenue of communication, clarification, and representation between itself and law enforcement so that public safety can be upheld and maintained."[2]

Currently, there are six members of the ACCPSAB, including two co-chairs. However, this initial group is considering bylaws that will define membership criteria and expectations. More members may be added later in 2021.[3]

The ACCPSAB meets monthly. At recent meetings, there have been presentations and discussions of the Special Victims Unit, Mental Health Unit, and Human Exploitation Unit[4] of the sheriff's office, as well as the school resource officer program.[5]

The ACCPSAB's website invites the public to "submit questions, concerns, or ideas for the board to review" through the general email address of the Alamance County Sheriff's office.

As of May 2021, the ACCPSAB is providing input on a public complaint form and developing its own bylaws.[6]

1. "Citizens' Public Safety Advisory Board," Alamance County Sheriff's Office, accessed May 24, 2021, https://www.alamance-nc.com/sheriff/programs/citizens-public-safety-advisory-board/.

2. Ibid.

3. Michelle Mills (Alamance County Sheriff's Office), in discussion with the author, May 26, 2021.

4. The Alamance County Citizens' Public Safety Advisory Board (ACCPSAB), *Alamance County Citizens' Public Safety Advisory Committee*, Overview 3-23-21, accessed May 26, 2021, https://www.alamance-nc.com/sheriff/wp-content/uploads/sites/25/2021/05/3-23-21-Citizens-Public-Safety-Review-Committee-Mtg-Overview.pdf.

5. Michelle Mills (Alamance County Sheriff's Office), in discussion with the author, May 26, 2021.

6. The board's agendas and minutes are available at https://www.alamance-nc.com/sheriff/citizens-public-safety-advisory-board/.

## The Asheville Citizens/Police Advisory Committee (CPAC)

The Asheville Citizens/Police Advisory Committee (CPAC) was originally founded in 1989 as a temporary group tasked with studying the relationship between the community and the police department. It was later granted status as an official advisory board in 1991.[7]

Today, the CPAC acts as a liaison between the police department and the public. The CPAC's primary function is to disseminate information about current policing topics and make recommendations to the city council. The CPAC does not have the legal authority to view private records or change policies. The committee's most recent meeting occurred in early 2020. Recent agendas included discussions of new community engagement initiatives, such as "Coffee with a Cop" and town hall meetings. Members of the committee occasionally participate in team building exercises.[8]

The CPAC's publications include an annual report summarizing the year's accomplishments. The 2019 report emphasized the committee's goal to engage citizens in their districts.[9] The committee educated citizens on how to file official complaints and listened to their concerns about community/police relations. Moreover, the CPAC held outreach meetings in various community centers and churches in the area. Members gave presentations about crime statistics to the community. However, the CPAC's 2018 annual report recalled high levels of turnover in the group due to resignations and "controversial incidents that transpired in the community."[10] Members made efforts to reorganize by rotating meeting locations throughout the city to make meetings more accessible to residents. Reorganization efforts included creating an outline for a mediation program. The program would act similarly to a review board by giving both the aggrieved party and the police an opportunity to share their side of the story. The group would not have access to confidential information, as in other review boards across the state.

The CPAC is exploring a partnership with the Human Relations Commission of Asheville. In August 2020, the two groups crafted a memorandum of understanding that reiterated the scope of each group's work.[11] The document emphasized that the agreement does not limit the powers given by the council to

---

7. The Asheville Citizens/Police Advisory Committee (CPAC), Resolution 91-67, https://documentcloud.adobe.com/spodintegration/index.html?r=1&locale=en-us.

8. "Citizens/Police Advisory Committee," The City of Asheville, last updated October 2, 2020, https://www.ashevillenc.gov/department/city-clerk/boards-and-commissions/citizens-police-advisory-committee/. Information was obtained from the various links in the "Agendas and Documents" section of this webpage.

9. Asheville CPAC, *2019 Annual Report* (January 30, 2020), https://drive.google.com/drive/folders/1qZICo8jY0T9nyvUw1kdNEsrL9FiYotM6.

10. Asheville CPAC, *2018 Annual Report*. The report does not elaborate upon these incidents.

11. Human Relations Commission of Asheville, *Regular Meeting Minutes* (August 27, 2020).

each group individually, but it does acknowledge the overlap of their missions. The two groups hope to collaborate in the future.

The CPAC created a set of goals for 2020 that included a desire for all CPAC members to participate in Asheville's Citizen's Police Academy.[12] Members also want to attend racial equity trainings and develop mediation techniques in partnership with the police department.

Members' terms last three years. The CPAC consists of nine voting members, including five representatives from the north, south, east, west, and central parts of Asheville. The committee also has two at-large seats. A resident of property owned by the Housing Authority of the City of Asheville and a representative from the housing authority occupy the final two seats. There is a designated city council member who acts as a liaison and is an ex-officio member of the committee. Originally, members included a youth representative, a frontline cop, the police chief, and the chair of the Asheville-Buncombe Community Relations Council.[13] Over the years, the city council amended these requirements for membership in the CPAC to their current form.

The CPAC's meetings are usually held every month but were paused due to the COVID-19 pandemic. At the time of this publication, the committee's meetings are held virtually.

## The Benson Police Advisory Commission (PAC)

The Town of Benson has had a Police Advisory Commission (PAC) since 2009. Its purposes are to "[r]epresent the point of view of the citizens of Benson," "review and provide a community perspective and recommendations concerning [law enforcement] programs and procedures," "enhance police-community relations," and promote public awareness of the Town's police services and programs.[14]

Benson Chief of Police Greg Percy has worked with PAC since 2015, when he was a captain of the city's police department. Coordinating and supporting community events to promote strong community-law enforcement relations is a recurring part of the PAC's work. Other common topics are strategies for high-crime areas, speed limit enforcement and pedestrian safety, neighborhood community watch, nuisance abatement, animal control matters, and opioid

---

12. For more information about this program, see https://www.ashevillenc.gov/service/sign-up-for-the-citizens-police-academy/.

13. This information was obtained from several Asheville CPAC resolutions, including Resolutions 91-67 (1991), 94-107 (1994), 94-186 (1994), 96-79 (1996), 11-1 (2011), 15-134 (2015), 16-124 (2016), and 19-128 (2019). See https://drive.google.com/file/d/1h9zC31FrNU2S_tZYoUu4qtYE9BWjwh3Q/view.

14. "Police Advisory Commission," Town of Benson, accessed February 22, 2021, https://www.townofbenson.com/2169/Police-Advisory-Commission.

overdose response. Some specific incidents (e.g., shootings, breaking and entering) are discussed by the PAC.

Information about hiring, training, and promotion of police personnel is reported to the PAC. The PAC holds no disciplinary or investigative powers and is not involved in operations of or oversight of the police department.

The PAC consists of six civilians appointed by the Benson Board of Commissioners and one elected commissioner representative. PAC chooses its chair and vice-chair. The ordinance establishing PAC calls for members to do police ride-alongs at least twice a year, with a two-hour minimum per ride along.[15] Chief Percy reports a good mix of members (an attorney, mental health counselor, a link to a member of local media), which ensures a wide range of viewpoints and expertise.

The PAC meets quarterly to discuss ideas for activities for community engagement with the Benson Police Department. One initiative for 2021 is outreach to seasonal (often agricultural) workers through churches and the Farm Bureau to build a supportive law enforcement relationship with all parts of Benson.

## The Burlington Community Police Advisory Team (CPAT)

In the summer and fall of 2020, the Burlington City Council and Mayor of Burlington initiated the charter process for the Burlington Community Police Advisory Team (CPAT). In response to local, regional, and national dialogue about policing, the city decided to move forward with a community-based team to advise the police chief and city manager. This team was the rekindling and reconstituting of a Chief's Advisory Committee in Burlington that stopped meeting in early 2016 due to poor attendance. Although the relationship between the Burlington community and the Burlington Police Department has been robust, city leaders believed mid-to-late 2020 was an opportune time to formalize a community-based advisory approach, with elected officials involved in the appointment of members, like the city's other boards and commissions.[16]

On February 2, 2021, the city council approved the charter for the group, designating the CPAT as an advisory board to the chief of police through the city manager.[17]

The CPAT's goal is to suggest new policies to the chief of police to foster a more collaborative relationship between the Burlington Police Department and the public. In February and March of 2021, the city council appointed eighteen members, following an application process that was widely advertised in the community. Two CPAT meetings were conducted in March 2021, including an

---

15. Benson Police Advisory Commission (PAC), *PAC Minutes* (February 27, 2012).

16. Hardin Watkins (Burlington City Manager), in discussion with the author, March 30, 2021.

17. "Community Police Advisory Team," Burlington, North Carolina, accessed March 23, 2021, https://nc-burlington3.civicplus.com/2163/Community-Police-Advisory-Team.

introductory meeting and a "meet and greet" for the members of the CPAT. The city is continuing recruitment for one or two youth members.[18]

The CPAT does not hold hearings or see evidence for individual cases. The team has a wide range of functions as a tool for community engagement and as an advisory board to the police chief and city manager. The CPAT's tasks include

- making recommendations to the police chief about training policies and diverse recruitment initiatives,
- reviewing and recommending policy enhancements,
- analyzing existing police department public records to help improve perception of procedural justice and enhance trust of police, and
- assisting with identification of policing best practices.[19]

The CPAT is an important part of maintaining Burlington's status per the Commission on Accreditation for Law Enforcement Agencies (CALEA). Burlington has held this accreditation in good standing for twenty-seven years and was recently reaccredited with the designation of Advanced Gold Standard in 2017.[20] CPAT will assist in components of accreditation through the review of annual reports on use of force, traffic stops, pursuits, and community relations metrics. The group also works to educate the public on police policies.

The CPAT aims to have about twenty members, which will be selected by the city council. Members must reside in Burlington and be representative of the population. Those who have been convicted of a misdemeanor or felony are still eligible to serve. The CPAT's charter lists a wide range of groups and employers from which to draw members as part of seeking a diverse set of members that reflects the community. Among the groups listed are members of all faith communities; Hispanic/Latinx, LGBTQ, and African-American communities; K-12 and community college personnel; members of the NAACP; youth, mental health, and business communities; and one "line level police employee."[21] Members are encouraged, but not required, to participate in a ride-along with a police officer, complete Burlington's Community Police Academy, or attend other group educational activities while completing their three-year term.[22]

The CPAT plans to meet monthly. The list of members and 2021 meeting dates are available online.[23] Additional meetings may be held in response to a police

18. Hardin Watkins (Burlington City Manager), in discussion with the author, March 30, 2021.
19. The Burlington Police Department, *Community Police Advisory Team Formation and Charter* Article IV, 2. (Burlington, NC: January 26, 2021), https://www.burlingtonnc.gov/DocumentCenter/View/19109/BPD-CPAT-Charter-Revised-020221?bidId= (adopted February 2, 2021).
20. "Police Reform Resources," Burlington Police Department, accessed April 30, 2021, http://www.burlingtonnc.gov/2113/Police-Reform-Resources.
21. The Burlington Police Department, *Community Police Advisory Team*.
22. Ibid., 5–6.
23. For a list of CPAT's members and meeting dates (as of April 30, 2021), see https://burlingtonnc.gov/2163/Community-Police-Advisory-Team.

shooting or in-custody death. As part of the CPAT charter, the city manager and chief of police must maintain membership in the National Association of Civilian Oversight for Law Enforcement (NACOLE) on behalf of Burlington. CPAT's charter was first established by the city council on November 17, 2020, and was amended on February 2, 2021, to better define the team's four categories of membership.[24]

## The Chapel Hill Community Policing Advisory Committee (CPAC)

The Chapel Hill Community Policing Advisory Committee (CPAC) was formed in 2011, following a 2008 citizens' petition. In response to the petition, a Chapel Hill Town Council subcommittee deliberated on what type of advisory body to create.

Appointments to the nine-member CPAC are made by the mayor and town council. Members of the CPAC serve three-year terms. A staff liaison is designated by the city manager.

The CPAC's responsibilities are to

- [m]ake recommendations to the Town Manager and Chief of Police with regard to organizational matters and procedures[;]
- [s]erve as a liaison to enhance community and police relations[;]
- [p]articipate in [the] annual review of the Police Department's Citizen Academy[;]
- [r]eceive, review, and consult on the quarterly professional standards report[;]
- [c]onsult and advise on the Police Department's strategic plan[;] and
- [p]rovide an annual report to Council on a Council requested topic.[25]

In August 2020, the CPAC held community outreach and listening sessions in response to the protests in Chapel Hill and in many other communities following the killing of George Floyd. One result of this engagement was to renew a commitment to diversify the CPAC with perspectives and experiences from certain segments of the community. The CPAC specifically identified marginalized populations (e.g., Black, Latinx, etc.) and lower-income groups as the main parts of the community whose voices needed greater attention.[26]

In Fall 2020, the CPAC formed three subcommittees to sharpen its work: community outreach, community safety implementation, and community safety data acquisition and analysis. A current focus is police and safety-related data analysis, with some CPAC members having expertise in this area. The CPAC

---

24. Hardin Watkins (Burlington City Manager), in discussion with the author, March 30, 2021.

25. Chapel Hill Town Council, *A Resolution to Establish a Community Policing Advisory Committee for the Town of Chapel Hill (2011-03-28/R-9)* (March 28, 2011), http://chapelhill.granicus.com/MetaViewer.php?view_id=&clip_id=975&meta_id=114560.

26. Joshua Romero (Chapel Hill CPAC Co-Chair), email to author, February 22, 2021.

anticipates using this analysis to form recommendations on transparency and how Chapel Hill reports about policing statistics.[27]

## The Charlotte Citizens' Review Board (CCRB)

The Charlotte Citizens' Review Board (CCRB) was created under city statutory authority in June 1997.[28] The board reviews complaints from citizens not satisfied with the outcomes of internal investigations of sworn officers of the Charlotte-Mecklenburg Police Department (CMPD). Charlotte is one of four localities in North Carolina with permission to disclose limited personnel information to CCRB members; this power was granted by state statute. The North Carolina General Assembly gave the CCRB the legal authority to view sensitive information in July 1997. CCRB may appeal decisions in cases of an injury, unlawful search and seizure, arrest, unbecoming conduct, use of force, or profiling. The CCRB reviews any discharge of a firearm that results in the death or injury of a person. The person injured or the next of kin may file the complaint. If there is no next of kin, city council members may file on the deceased's behalf.[29]

The CCRB's responsibilities include acting as an advisory board to the chief of police, city council, and city manager. Each year, the group produces a report discussing the year's cases and accomplishments, as well as providing recommendations for the Charlotte-Mecklenburg Community Relations Committee (CRC).[30]

Citizens file complaints through the CRC. The CCRB conducts a preliminary hearing, and if there is sufficient evidence of error, a secondary hearing takes place. The secondary hearing acts as a fact-finding process through which the CCRB examines additional evidence, hears from witnesses, and allows cross examinations from both the complainant and the CMPD. At the conclusion of the hearing, the CCRB summarizes the findings into a report for the chief of police and the city manager.

The CCRB's Fiscal Year 2019 report included accomplishments from a subcommittee of the board that recommended changes to the CMPD's use of force policy. The report also described upcoming events/discussions and provided additional recommendations to the city council.[31] In 2018, CCRB gathered a list

---

27. Joshua Romero (Chapel Hill CPAC Co-Chair), email correspondence with author, February 1–22, 2021.

28. Charlotte, NC, Code Ch. 16, Art. II, § 16-56 (1997).

29. S.L. 1997-305.

30. For examples of these reports, see https://charlottenc.gov/CityClerk/Pages/Citizens ReviewBoard.aspx.

31. Charlotte Citizens' Review Board (CCRB), *2018–2019 Annual Report*, https:// charlottenc.gov/CityClerk/Documents/2018-2019%20CRB%20Annual%20Report.pdf.

of attorneys willing to represent low-income citizens in appeals pro bono.[32] The board also participates in workshops on subjects like implicit bias.[33]

Annual reports on the CCRB's website list the outcomes concerning appeals and hearings from 2012–2019 (see Table 1).

## Table 1. CCRB Appeals and Hearings Outcomes from 2012–2019

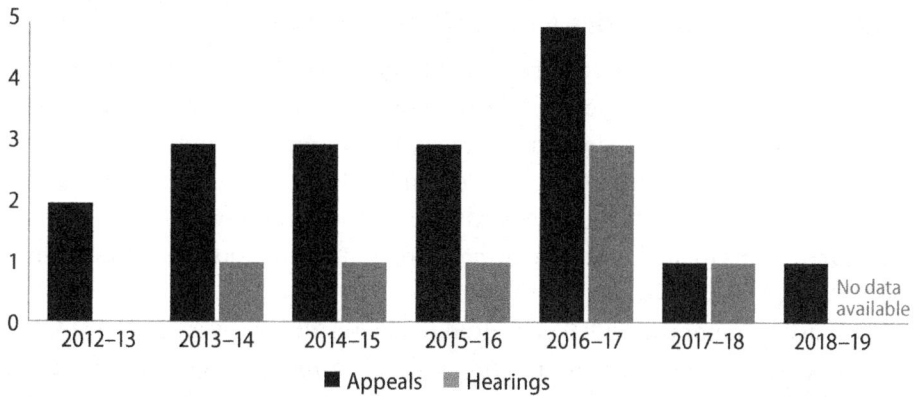

*Source*: "Citizens Review Board," City of Charlotte, https://charlottenc.gov/CityClerk/Pages/Citizens ReviewBoard.aspx.

The city manager makes the final decision on whether or not the complaint warrants disciplinary action against police.

Eleven members serve on the CCRB. Three members are appointed by the mayor, five members are appointed by the city council, and three members are appointed by the city manager. Prospective members must meet several requirements for acceptance, including passing an interview process with the city council, city manager, and CRC. Members must be permanent residents of the county and registered to vote in the county. Current and former employees of the county are not eligible for membership. Current and former CMPD officers, as well as their spouses, parents, or children, may not serve on the board. Persons that have committed certain misdemeanors are ineligible for membership.[34]

Prospective members must complete the CMPD's Citizens' Academy and receive training on relevant legal, policy, and cultural awareness issues, as

---

32. CCRB, *2017–2018 Annual Report*, https://charlottenc.gov/CityClerk/Documents /2017-2018%20CRB%20Annual%20Report_F.pdf.

33. CCRB, *2016–2017 Annual Report*, https://charlottenc.gov/CityClerk/Documents /2016-2017%20CRB%20Annual%20Report.pdf.

34. "Citizens Review Board," City of Charlotte, https://charlottenc.gov/CityClerk/Pages /CitizensReviewBoard.aspx.

required by the city manager, before they can participate in board activities.[35] Current members must complete eight hours of continuing education training each year. Training may include a four-hour ride-along with a CMPD officer. Accepted members must sign a confidentiality agreement[36] regarding all confidential information, as dictated by city, county, and/or state laws.[37]

## The Durham Civilian Police Review Board (CPRB)

The Durham Civilian Police Review Board (CPRB) was established by state law in 1998.[38] CPRB receives appeals of determinations made by the Durham Police Department's Professional Standards Division (hereinafter Professional Standards Division) after investigations of actions taken by Durham police officers have been completed. The Professional Standards Division initially investigates these complaints. If unsatisfied with the outcome of an investigation, a complainant may file a request for a hearing with the CPRB.[39]

The jurisdiction of the CPRB is limited to the results of investigations of use of force; unethical conduct and/or conduct unbecoming of police department personnel; or arrest, search, and seizure.[40] The CPRB has handled sixty-eight appeal requests in some form in the period of 1999 to 2020.

The CPRB focuses on whether there was improper use of discretion during the police department's conduct of an investigation. The CPRB examines written evidence submitted by the complainant and conducts a review of the investigatory file generated by the Professional Standards Division to determine whether a hearing should be held. The board first determines if a hearing is justified, and, if so, conducts a hearing. Following the hearing, the board's findings are submitted to the city manager for follow-up and additional response.

CPRB members are appointed by the Durham city manager and confirmed by the city council. The nine-member board meets quarterly (unless workload calls for additional meetings) and includes a chair and vice chair. Members serve

---

35. For more information about the Charlotte-Mecklenburg Police Department's Citizens' Academy, see https://charlottenc.gov/CMPD/Organization/Pages/AdminSvcs/Training Academy/Citizens_Academy.aspx.

36. Confidentiality pledges or signed documents affirm that civilian review board (CRB) members must protect the integrity of their review of complaints about police conduct are common for all CRBs in North Carolina.

37. City of Charlotte, "Citizens Review Board."

38. S.L. 1998-142 (SB 1509).

39. City of Durham, *How to File a Complaint Against the Durham Police Department and Request a Review*, https://durhamnc.gov/DocumentCenter/View/11619/cprb-brochure-revised_final-print.

40. Durham Civilian Police Review Board (CPRB), *FY 2014-2015 Annual Report*, 4, https://durhamnc.gov/ArchiveCenter/ViewFile/Item/2374.

four-year, staggered terms and are eligible for re-appointment. The city attorney's office provides a liaison to CPRB.

New members must complete a comprehensive training program (which covers eleven topics, delivered by staff from the City Manager's Office, City Attorney's Office, and Durham Police Department) to be eligible to participate in a hearing. Other requirements are sixteen hours in a patrol car ride-along across the first year as a member and completion of the police department's Citizens Police Academy program.

In 2014, the Durham City Council amended the Civilian Police Review Board Procedure Manual to

a. lengthen the period a citizen has for filing a request for CPRB review (to thirty business days);
b. require the CPRB to host one community forum per fiscal year to hear feedback about the Durham Police Department complaint process and community-police relations; and
c. require the CPRB to make at least two educational presentations to community, civic, or neighborhood groups per fiscal year.[41]

The CPRB has produced annual reports since 2000.[42] The reports include the number of meetings and attendance of board members. Reports list the names of people requesting board review of their complaint and if those requests proceeded to a CPRB hearing. For example, in the 2011–2012 report, four cases were brought by complainants, and the board voted in each case not to proceed to a hearing.[43] In 2014–2015, seven complaints led to two appeals hearings. One complaint concerned allegations of improper search and seizure, and the other (involving three complainants from the same family) concerned allegations of improper use of force (both hearings occurred in the following fiscal year).[44]

In the majority of cases, the CPRB does not grant a hearing to the complainant; in fifty-four of the sixty-eight cases in the period of October 1999–August 2020, a hearing was not granted to the complainant.[45]

The annual reports sometimes note other concerns. For example, the 2002–2003 annual report "expressed concern about procedures related to the identification requirements imposed on off-duty officers."[46] The 2008–2009 report expressed "concerns about the small number of cases presented to the Board over the last few years."[47] The report also discussed the board's visibility

---

41. Ibid., 2.

42. Annual reports since 2012 are available online at https://durhamnc.gov/Archive.aspx?AMID=41.

43. Durham CPRB, *Annual Report July 1, 2011–June 30, 2012*, https://durhamnc.gov/ArchiveCenter/ViewFile/Item/208.

44. Durham CPRB, *FY 2014–2015 Annual Report*.

45. Durham CPRB, *Request for Appeals Hearings*.

46. Durham CPRB, *Annual Report July 1, 2002–June 30, 2003*.

47. Durham CPRB, *Annual Report July 1, 2008–June 30, 2009*, 2.

on the city's website, requested a link be placed on the police department's website, and explained how the distinction of the CPRB reporting to the city manager rather than the city council is "not meaningful to a citizen wishing to find information" about the CPRB.[48] For two years in a row, CPRB expressed concern about the timeliness of complaints being investigated by the Professional Standards Division.[49]

The CPRB website includes links to how to file an appeal, a set of frequently asked questions, the board's procedure manual, and the application to become a CPRB member. The Civilian Police Review Board Procedure Manual was initially approved by the Durham City Council in 2003 and was amended in 2014 and 2019.[50]

## The Durham County Sheriff's Community Advisory Board (CAB)

In August 2019, Durham County Sheriff Clarence F. Birkhead established the Sheriff's Community Advisory Board (CAB). Sheriff Birkhead's goal was to have the CAB "serve as the voice of the community by presenting issues, suggesting ideas and offering advice" and "build trust and create a positive working relationship between Durham County Sheriff's Office (DCSO) and the larger Durham County community."[51]

In selecting CAB members, Sheriff Birkhead was careful to include people from various zip codes throughout Durham County. He also required that members

- reside in Durham and be at least 21 years of age;
- have the ability to
    - listen and engage with people from different cultures and socioeconomic backgrounds with varying opinions,
    - think independently and work collaboratively,
    - think critically,
    - ask and answer questions,
    - understand issues from different perspectives, and
    - understand and process information (print, online, and oral) effectively and efficiently; and
- demonstrate open-mindedness, curiosity, responsiveness, and willingness to work with others.

48. Ibid.
49. Durham CPRB, 2009–10 and 2010–11 annual reports.
50. City of Durham, *Civilian Police Review Board Procedure Manual* (approved by Durham City Council on September 2, 2003; revised November 17, 2014; revised June 3, 2019), https://durhamnc.gov/DocumentCenter/View/956/Civilian-Police-Review-Board-Procedure-Manual-PDF.
51. "Building Trust between Law Enforcement & Community, Sheriff Birkhead Launches 'Community Advisory Board'", *Durham County, NC, News*, August 16, 2019, https://www.dconc.gov/Home/Components/News/News/6214/31.

Upon appointment, members attend the Durham Sheriff's Community Academy to learn and understand the operations and responsibilities of the DCSO. Members must also sign a confidentiality agreement.

The Durham Sheriff CAB's responsibilities include:

- informing the sheriff of community issues or concerns,
- offering ideas and suggestions to address and resolve community concerns,
- advising the sheriff on how to improve community trust between law enforcement and their respective communities,
- uncovering blind spots that are evident to the community but not necessarily specific to law enforcement,
- informing the community of important initiatives and bringing feedback to the sheriff, and
- maintaining the confidentiality of all closed meetings and information acquired as a board member.[52]

The CAB's meeting minutes are sent annually to the Commission on Accreditation for Law Enforcement Agencies, Inc. (CALEA).[53]

As an elected official, Sheriff Birkhead is bound by North Carolina's constitutional statutes, which guide all sheriff offices in the state. He may not transfer his administrative duties to an individual or an advisory board. Consequently, the CAB may suggest or recommend, but final authority or action rests with the sheriff.

The CAB first met in November 2019, with a goal of meeting quarterly. The first meeting was an orientation that was meant to describe the CAB's role and responsibilities. In February 2020, the CAB members attended the Durham Sheriff's Community Academy (a thirty-two-hour introduction to the operations of the Durham Sheriff's Office) over a four-week period. The COVID-19 pandemic interfered with the April 2020 meeting, but after making arrangements to meet virtually, meetings were held in May, July, September, and November 2020. In December, the CAB convened to determine members' commitment to remain on the board for an additional year. A majority of members were pleased to serve for another year.[54]

The Durham Sheriff's Office's director of community engagement, Grace Marsh, supports the work of the CAB by preparing agendas and materials for meetings, responding to information requests by CAB members, and conducting research as requested by the sheriff. Sheriff Birkhead's CAB drew on the work of the President's Task Force of 21st Century Policing in its final report[55] and expanded research on civilian law enforcement boards across the country.

---

52. Ibid.

53. Grace Marsh (Durham County Sheriff's Office Director of Community Engagement), email correspondence with author, December 2020–April 2021.

54. Ibid.

55. The report can be found here: https://cops.usdoj.gov/pdf/taskforce/taskforce_finalreport.pdf.

Birkhead's goal is to hear directly from Durham community members up close and personal.[56]

## The Greensboro Criminal Justice Advisory Commission (GCJAC) and the Police Community Review Board (PCRB)

### Overview of Greensboro's Review Boards

Greensboro has two civilian bodies that provide oversight of police and other parts of the criminal justice system. The Greensboro Criminal Justice Advisory Commission (GCJAC) is a nine-member body, appointed by the Greensboro City Council, which reports directly to the Greensboro City Council and the City Manager's Office. It was established in August 2018. In 2001, consistent with the review of complaints made about police conduct, a North Carolina General Assembly law permitted the disclosure of limited personnel information on the disposition of police disciplinary charges against police officers;[57] this law now supports the work of the Greensboro Police Community Review Board (PCRB).

According to the GCJAC's website, the commission's purpose is to (1) "identify, address and monitor issues"; (2) "[e]ducate and advocate for the public by hosting forums on various justice-related topics and studying trends in policing strategies within the Greensboro Police Department (GPD)"; (3) "provid[e] perspective on policies that affect the public's interaction with law enforcement";[58] and (4) provide recommendations to the city and the GPD on how to address issues.[59]

The PCRB is a subcommittee of the GCJAC. The PCRB reviews complaints filed against members of the GPD **after** those complaints have been investigated and ruled upon by the department's Professional Standards Division. "The PCRB's goal is to provide positive advisory determinations and/or recommendations of how residents are treated in interactions with officers and how that can improve in the future."[60]

The GCJAC's website emphasizes that "[n]either PCRB nor GCJAC investigate any GPD complaints."[61] The GCJAC also has subcommittees that address matters concerning policy and education/outreach.[62]

56. Grace Marsh (Durham County Sheriff's Office Director of Community Engagement), email correspondence with author, December 2020–April 2021.

57. S.L. 2001-20.

58. "Greensboro Criminal Justice Advisory Commission (GCJAC)," Greensboro, North Carolina, accessed May 17, 2021, https://www.greensboro-nc.gov/departments/legislative /greensboro-criminal-justice-advisory-commission.

59. GCJAC, *Annual Report 2019-2020* (June 2020), 3, https://www.greensboro-nc.gov/home /showpublisheddocument/47545/637431951003100000.

60. Ibid., 6.

61. Greensboro, North Carolina, "Greensboro Criminal Justice Advisory Commission (GCJAC)."

62. GCJAC, *Annual Report 2019-2020*.

## The Greensboro Police Community Review Board (PCRB): Scope, Structure, and Actions

The Greensboro Police Community Review Board's (PCRB) charge was updated in 2018 to hear all appeals of complaints of employee misconduct in violation of department directives made against sworn officers of the GPD and to review other complaints as necessary in support of the GCJAC's responsibility to monitor, review, and analyze issues related to the police disciplinary process.[63]

The PCRB is comprised of seven members. Four of the members are drawn from the GCJAC. Those members are appointed by the chair of the GCJAC. The remaining three members are appointed by the mayor, with the concurrence of the city council.

The PCRB meets at least quarterly, and members must maintain confidentiality of material related to the investigation and disposition of a person's complaint about police conduct. Extensive rules of procedure guide their review of the police department's investigation of a complaint. In addition to standards for confidentiality and member conflict of interest, members receive an orientation and training through the city attorney's office and the police department. The training includes the following topics: cultural competencies, police standard operating procedures, and legal and statutory considerations.[64]

Every decision of the PCRB must be supported by stated findings of fact and legal conclusions adequate to explain the basis of the decision but cannot contain any facts or legal conclusions that are confidential information contained in the police officer's personnel file.

A decision of the PCRB may include a recommendation to the chief of police and the city manager for the revision or adoption of a policy or disposition of disciplinary charges. If the PCRB issues a written determination that disagrees with the Division of Professional Standards, the PCRB may hold a conference with the chief of police. If the PCRB and chief of police cannot resolve any matter of disagreement, the PCRB may issue a written notice of continued appeal to the city manager and provide all information related to the case to the city manager for further action. After review, the city manager will provide a decision concerning the matter in writing, which shall be final. If the PCRB disagrees with the decision of the city manager, the PCRB may issue a written notice of the basis of its disagreement to the city manager and the chair of the GCJAC.[65]

The PCRB publishes annual information on resident complaints against police, not just for cases reviewed by the PCRB.[66] The individual instances are listed with an action of either unfounded, sustained, not sustained, and exonerated. There

---

63. *Rules of Procedure of the Police Community Review Board*, 1. (Report was obtained by author from an inquiry to staff contact on May 19, 2021.)

64. *Rules of Procedure of the Police Community Review Board*, 3.

65. *Rules of Procedure of the Police Community Review Board*, 10.

66. For example, see the board's data from 2019 here: https://www.greensboro-nc.gov/Home /ShowDocument?id=46181.

is also a mediation option, which does not report the outcome of the mediation. Between October 2019 and October 2020, five appeals came to the PCRB. One was withdrawn, and the other four were "sustained," meaning the PCRB found that GPD took appropriate actions in investigating the complaint.

### The Greensboro Criminal Justice Advisory Commission (GCJAC)

At the request of the city council, the GCJAC reviewed the police department's consent to search policy. Overall, the GCJAC found the policy to be "very comprehensive" and that it "allows for a great level of transparency."[67] The GCJAC recommended that officers "should obtain voluntary consent from those persons (1) by verbally informing them of their right to refuse a search and (2) by securing written consent through the GPD Consent to Search form."[68]

The GCJAC addressed hemp and marijuana similarities related to police searches and recommended that "[a]s marijuana and hemp are indistinguishable from each other by field tests, the presence of the odor of hemp or marijuana should not be used as a reason for probable cause to search."[69] The GCJAC added that marijuana violations should be deprioritized. In 2019, the Restraint Review Subcommittee of GCJAC met with the GPD's Restraint Review Committee to address procedures and devices to be used when dealing with individuals that are in an extremely agitated state. The memo from the GCJAC Restraint Review Subcommittee states that "the consensus was that restraining the individual should be done as quickly as possible using minimal restraints."[70]

In response to the killing of George Floyd and the resulting protests, the GCJAC chair posted an open letter reminding Greensboro residents of the goals of the GCJAC and that "[d]uring these turbulent times the GCJAC is here to support the Greensboro community and create space for dialog and solution driven conversations."[71]

The GCJAC creates annual reports, which include information about member meeting attendance, GPD complaints by kind and outcomes of the Professional Standards Division's investigations, and GCJAC goals for the coming year. The GCJAC's 2019–2020 report identified addressing traffic stops and conducting community outreach and education efforts for residents to understand "their rights and how to interact with law enforcement" as goals for 2020–21.[72]

---

67. For the full report, see https://www.greensboro-nc.gov/Home/ShowDocument?id=45981.

68. GCJAC, *Annual Report 2019-2020*, 14.

69. Recommendation from the GCJAC on hemp versus marijuana (on file with author).

70. GCJAC, *Memorandum*, https://www.greensboro-nc.gov/home/showpublisheddocument/47318/637401906005970000.

71. For the full letter from Jaye Webb, the GCJAC chair as of June 1, 2020, see https://www.greensboro-nc.gov/home/showdocument?id=45879.

72. GCJAC, *Annual Report 2019-2020*, 11.

## The Greenville Police Community Relations Committee (PCRC)

Greenville's Police Community Relations Committee (PCRC) was created in 1996. The main functions of the committee are "[t]o serve as [a] liaison between [the] community and police over concerns" and "to serve as [an] advocate for programs, ideas, and methods to improve relationships between the community and the Greenville Police Department."[73] The group disseminates information regarding the state of policing practices in the city. It also prioritizes educating citizens on public safety issues and individual awareness.

The committee's most recent meeting agendas include a discussion of police policy reforms, during which the chief of police solicited advice from the committee on how to get community feedback on current police policies.[74] In February 2020, the PCRC invited students from East Carolina University to discuss police relations with students. The group discussed expectations for future interactions and made efforts to dispel harmful assumptions about the other party.[75] Individual PCRC members have also planned their own outreach and educational events. Topics for these events have included neighborhood policing and post-arrest rehabilitation.[76] The group also brings in guest speakers to discuss topics such as methods to decrease recidivism among repeat offenders.

The PCRC consists of seven members appointed by the Greenville City Council. Five of those individuals represent each of the five districts of the city; the remaining two positions are occupied by one individual chosen by the city council member at-large and one chosen by the mayor. In addition to the seven appointed members, the police chief and a police attorney are included in the PCRC as ex-officio advisors. Members can serve two terms. Each December, the committee elects a chairperson and a vice chairperson, who each serve one year. The PCRC meets monthly, except for July and August. This meeting frequency excludes special meetings called by the chairperson in the case of the occurrence of an event of interest to the community.

Members of the PCRC must abide by the PCRC's code of conduct.[77] They must commit to acting in a nonpartisan fashion, regularly updating the council member who appointed them of their contributions, and actively pursuing feedback from citizens. Members also commit to not publicly share their views on

73. "Police Community Relations Committee," Greenville, North Carolina, accessed May 18, 2021, https://www.greenvillenc.gov/government/police/police-community-relations-committee.

74. Greenville Police Community Relations Committee (PCRC), *Summary Minutes for the Police Community Relations Committee*, February 12, 2019, https://www.greenvillenc.gov /home/showdocument?id=18723.

75. Greenville PCRC, *Summary Minutes for the Police Community Relations Committee*, February 11, 2020. A Word document of these meeting minutes can be found here: https:// www.greenvillenc.gov/government/city-council/boards-and-commissions/police-community -relations-committee/2020-police-community-relations-committee-meeting-schedule-and -agendas.

76. Ibid.

77. Greenville PCRC, *Code of Conduct*, 4.

PCRC matters to avoid the appearance of representing the committee as a whole. Committee members must be residents of the City of Greenville.

## Guilford County Sheriff's Community Roundtable

In response to the Summer 2020 protests following law enforcement actions in Kentucky and Minnesota, Guilford County Sheriff Danny Rogers invited residents to serve on a community roundtable. The roundtable serves as a sounding board for community concerns and for Sheriff Rogers to inform the community about the functions of his department, as well as discuss with the community those functions and the issues Rogers sees for effective sheriff-community relations.[78]

Many people responded to the open call to serve on the roundtable. An internal Guilford County Sheriff's Office group reviewed the applications and recommended an initial twenty-five members, who first met via online video in July 2020. Between August and October, about seven more people were added as members.[79]

The sheriff sought diversity of membership. Rogers aimed to include people on the roundtable from both large cities in Guilford County, High Point and Greensboro, as well as other communities in the county. He also sought diversity of race and gender on the roundtable, and he indicated his plan to select at least one roundtable member from each of the following groups:

- [l]ocal religious community leaders/clerics[,]
- [the] NAACP[,]
- [a]dvocates for those with special needs and persons with disabilities[,]
- [the] Chamber of Commerce[,]
- [s]chools[,] [and]
- [the] LGBTQ community.[80]

Representatives were also sought from health-care agencies, nonprofits, and advocacy groups.[81]

The roundtable has met monthly (except for the period of November 2020–January 2021); typically, the meetings involve a speaker from the Guilford County Sheriff's Office to discuss a particular function or challenge.

---

78. "Sheriff's Roundtable Group," Guilford County, State of North Carolina, accessed April 28, 2021, https://www.guilfordcountync.gov/our-county/sheriff-s-office/communications/sheriff-s-roundtable-group.

79. Lori Poag (Guilford County Sheriff's Office), in discussion with the author, April 13, 2021.

80. Jamie Biggs, "Watch Now: Greensboro police chief modifies policies in wake of protests over George Floyd's death in Minneapolis," *Greensboro News and Record*, June 8, 2020, https://greensboro.com/news/local_news/watch-now-greensboro-police-chief-modifies-policies-in-wake-of-protests-over-george-floyds-death/article_70ce0a6b-aa88-52bc-b8c6-bd9ab14ee7bb.html.

81. "Sheriff's Roundtable Group," Guilford County, State of North Carolina.

For the March 2021 meeting, a leader in the Legal Process Division of the sheriff's office presented and answered questions about the big increase in handgun permits, especially for concealed carry, and how his division is using retirees and other staff to reduce a backlog of applications. After the speaker gives a presentation, the sheriff and other staff respond to questions and concerns of the members.

So far, no formal notes or minutes of roundtable meetings are kept. The Guilford County Sheriff's Office's communication specialist, Lori Poag, facilitates the group by managing the online meeting arrangements and responding to members who miss a meeting with a summary of what happened.

With anticipated changes in COVID-19 restrictions, Sheriff Rogers hopes to have the first face-to-face meeting of the roundtable in June 2021.[82]

## The Knightdale Community Policing Advisory Board (CPAB)

From 2015–2018, a police advisory board operated in Knightdale. In 2018, the Knightdale Town Council created a Public Safety Advisory Board (PSAB), which focused on fire and police services. In fall 2020, the Knightdale Town Council decided to divide the PSAB into two boards: (1) a board for the town's fire services, which was called the "Fire Service Advisory Board" and (2) a board for the town's police services, which was called the "Community Policing Advisory Board" (CPAB). The CPAB was formally created in January 2021.[83]

The CPAB is made up of five members serving staggered two-year terms. As with all Knightdale citizen advisory boards,[84] CPAB members must abide by the town's code of ethics for residents serving on advisory boards.[85]

The CPAB's duties include promoting educational and outreach activities and providing input on police policies and practices, including possible specific recommendations to the Knightdale Police Chief. CPAB members are expected to (1) serve as liaisons to enhance community and police relations and (2) assist with the review of the Knightdale Police Department's Citizen Police Academy curriculum. Finally, members are to provide "reports, feedback and statements of support/opposition to the Town Council as required."[86]

---

82. Lori Poag (Guilford County Sheriff's Office), in discussion with the author, April 13, 2021.

83. Ordinance Creating a Community Policing Advisory Board ORD #21-01-20-001.

84. Knightdale has citizen advisory boards that address topics other than policing. For more information, see https://www.knightdalenc.gov/government/advisory-boards.

85. See the "Code of Ethics for Citizen Advisory Board Members of the Town of Knightdale, North Carolina" here: https://www.knightdalenc.gov/sites/default/files/uploads/nb_-_code_of_ethics_for_boards_and_committees_-_updated_draft.pdf.

86. "Community Policing Advisory Board," Knightdale, accessed March 1, 2021, https://www.knightdalenc.gov/government/advisory-boards/community-policing-advisory-board.

In July 2020, the PSAB was presented with a draft ordinance regulating golf carts. They voted unanimously to recommend that the town council adopt the ordinance.[87]

The PSAB's meetings that addressed matters affecting law enforcement in 2019 involved a discussion of revisions to the town's false alarms ordinance, examination of data on speeding complaints, and a presentation by the city manager explaining the public safety section of the town's annual budget. PSAB members were alerted to a forum on human trafficking, and the chief of police reviewed the 2018 year for service calls and crimes and compared the data to that of 2017.[88]

## Manteo Community-Police Advisory Board

As part of several changes to address police-community and police-business relations, Manteo Town Manager James Ayers and Police Chief Vance J. Haskett established the Manteo Community-Police Advisory Board in early 2021.[89] The Manteo Board of Commissioners appointed six residents to the board, and the first meeting was held in February 2021.

The Community-Police Advisory Board is intended to provide advice, feedback, and suggestions to the town's police department. Their work is part of the broader model of community policing. The desired outcomes are for a robust community partnership between the police and the Manteo community and for engagement of the police department and the Manteo community in joint problem-solving.[90]

The Community-Police Advisory Board meets quarterly. It is in the process of choosing a president and vice-president, and the board's most recent meeting was in May 2021.[91]

## The Morrisville Public Safety Advisory Committee (PSAC)

In 2013, the Morrisville Town Council established a Public Safety Advisory Committee (PSAC) with a broad mandate to advise the council on fire and police matters. The PSAC can comment on budget items; recommend policies in the

---

87. *Knightdale Public Safety Advisory Board Minutes* (July 9, 2020), 2, https://codelibrary.amlegal.com/codes/knightdale/latest/m/2020/7/9.

88. Chief Lawrence Capps (Knightdale Police), email correspondence with author, February–March 2021.

89. There was an earlier, informal advisory board, with members chosen by the previous chief of police, which operated roughly from 2000 to 2007.

90. "Community-Police Advisory Board," Town of Manteo, North Carolina, accessed April 21, 2021, https://www.manteonc.gov/government/boards-and-committees/community-police-advisory-board.

91. Ibid.

form of draft resolutions and ordinances; and generally "examine ideas and report on methods and concepts to protect and improve citizens' health, safety, and welfare and the peace and dignity of the Town."[92]

Appointed by the Morrisville Town Council, the eleven-member board chooses its chair and vice-chair. As of February 2021, eight members joined in 2019 for a two-year term. The other members are in either their second or third two-year term. There are no term limits for regular members. There is a two-term limit for a member filling either the chair or vice-chair position. The PSAC meets six times per year, and subcommittees meet as needed. Staff support for PSAC alternates annually between the Morrisville Police Department and Morrisville Fire Department.[93]

The PSAC makes recommendations on appeals of parking citations.[94] This appears to be the only civilian police advisory body in North Carolina that has this responsibility. People receiving parking tickets can make an appeal (online or in writing), which the PSAC reviews at their quarterly meetings. They review the accuracy and proper intention of the parking citation. About 95 percent of the appeals are denied. PSAC can consider recommendations on improved signage based on their review of parking citations.[95]

As of late 2020, the PSAC is considering creating a subcommittee on police reform. The police chief provided information and advice in fall 2020 concerning the establishment of such a committee. At present, it is undetermined if the subcommittee will review citizen complaints of officer conduct. In early 2021, the PSAC set a priority of improving pedestrian and bicycle safety as part of their 2021 Workplan.

Other recent topics addressed were policy on taser use and vehicle break-ins.[96] PSAC draws on the Morrisville Town Council's strategic plan and early in 2020 addressed increasing homeowner association involvement with PSAC and an information flyer.[97]

---

92. *Charter of the Morrisville Public Safety Advisory Committee* (April 13, 2013), https:// boule-us-production.s3.amazonaws.com/uploads/production/board_answer/attachment /129059/Public_Safety_Advisory_Committee_Charter_2013.02.18.pdf?X-Amz-Expires=60&X -Amz-Date=20210621T133407Z&X-Amz-Algorithm=AWS4-HMAC-SHA256&X-Amz-Creden tial=AKIATHOFOHMMBRNFRBE2/20210621/us-east-1/s3/aws4_request&X-Amz-Signed Headers=host&X-Amz-Signature=42e074660e54491fde6bc48a8e6f339dc9956a7675d305cd6a4 7521689dadafe.

93. Bill Granger (Morrisville Fire Department), in discussion with author, February 23, 2021.

94. This information was drawn from the Morrisville Public Safety Advisory Committee's (PSAC) minutes of its October 6, 2020, meeting.

95. Bill Granger (Morrisville Fire Department), in discussion with author, February 23, 2021.

96. Ibid.

97. *Update SMART Objectives for PSAC* (February 14, 2020).

## The New Bern Police Civil Service Board (PCSB)

New Bern established the New Bern Police Civil Service Board (PCSB) as early as 1957.[98] The PCSB's purpose was to partner with the New Bern Police Department in the hiring process for police officers and to serve as an appeals board for officers facing disciplinary or termination actions.

The PCSB's advising role in the hiring process was an unusual form of civilian influence on local policing and was ended in 2016. The board continues its work on appeals of officers facing disciplinary or termination actions. However, this type of appeals function does not fit the definition of citizen advisory or review activity described in this book, so it can be considered that the PCSB's advisory function ended in 2016.

The New Bern Board of Aldermen makes appointments to the five-member board. A PCSB member must be a qualified voter and cannot be an employee of the city, a member of the Board of Aldermen, an elective officer, a member or employee of the police department, or a person who has served as a volunteer in the police department within the previous thirty-six months.[99]

The PCSB had a direct role in the New Bern Police Department hiring process from 1965 (possibly earlier) to 2016. There were different formats for guidance earlier in the board's existence, including managing competitive examinations and maintaining a register of those who passed the examination.[100] More recently, the PCSB became involved in the police department's hiring process after an applicant went through interviews with police department personnel. A second interview occurred with the PCSB, and the board made a recommendation about the applicant.[101]

In recent years, concerns were raised about the time the PCSB's review added to the process of evaluating applicants. New Bern City Council members and police leaders believed that some qualified candidates were not successful due to the longer hiring timeline. These concerns prompted a revision to the New Bern City Charter in June 2016 to remove the PCSB's involvement in hiring for the New Bern police department. The amendment also refined the qualifications of those who could be appointed to the PCSB.[102]

While the PCSB does continue to function for appeals by officers who have been suspended or terminated, this is a departure from the function of providing civilian input on grievances originating from residents, visitors, or business owners. There are various forms of civil service boards in North Carolina local government that conduct reviews of adverse actions taken by supervisors affecting their subordinates.

---

98. The exact date is uncertain; the board was operational no later than 1965, per S.L. 1965, Ch. 693 (HB 870).

99. New Bern Code of Ord., No. 19-003, § 2-108.

100. S.L. 1969, Ch. 324 (HB 578).

101. Scott Davis (New Bern Town Attorney), email message to author.

102. Ibid.

## The Raleigh Police Advisory Board (PAB)

Across the period of February through July 2020, the Raleigh City Council formed a Police Advisory Board (PAB). The PAB is a liaison between the Raleigh community and the Raleigh City Council. Its main goal is to "help build trust and relationships between the Raleigh Police Department and the community."[103]

The PAB has nine members, each serving a two-year term with a maximum of three terms. Several membership positions are designated by expertise or community connection, including

- mental-health provider,
- victim advocate,
- attorney, and
- member of the LGBT community.[104]

The Raleigh Police Department Police Chief appoints one member, and the city council appoints the other eight members, plus two alternates. Three members are "at-large." Members are required to undergo forty hours of orientation and training.[105] Members are listed on the PAB website.[106] The current PAB Chair is Sheila Alamin Khashoggi, and the primary staff contact is Dr. Audrea Caesar, Executive Director of the Raleigh Office of Equity and Inclusion.

The PAB's main responsibilities are to (1) review existing Raleigh Police Department procedures and contribute to fair policy development and (2) conduct educational outreach initiatives in order to engage community members in Raleigh Police Department directives.

The Raleigh PAB "will not conduct investigations, hear testimony, or contribute to disciplinary action. The board will not respond to citizen complaints. The board will not collect data. Any complaints received by the city will be shared with this board to drive their work prioritization."[107]

The PAB has met monthly since September 2020, with agendas and Zoom meeting recordings available online.[108] In spring 2021, the PAB discussed their role and community engagement in the search for a new chief of police.[109]

---

103. "Police Advisory Board," Raleigh, North Carolina, accessed April 30, 2021, https://raleighnc.gov/police-advisory-board.

104. Raleigh City Council, *Regular Meeting-Third Tuesday-Afternoon Session* (June 16, 2020), https://go.boarddocs.com/nc/raleigh/Board.nsf/goto?open&id=A4EMF95B00BF.

105. This information was obtained from a presentation by Marchell Adams-David (Raleigh City Manager) at the N.C. City Attorneys Conference webinar (March 25, 2021).

106. "Police Advisory Board," Raleigh, North Carolina.

107. Ibid.

108. The Raleigh Police Advisory Board's (PAB) meeting agendas and minutes, as well as Zoom recordings of the meetings, can be found here: https://go.boarddocs.com/nc/raleigh/Board.nsf/goto?open&id=BTJRHT6BCBE0.

109. These discussions are described in the Raleigh PAB's meeting minutes for March 24, 2021 and for April 28, 2021, which can be found here: https://go.boarddocs.com/nc/raleigh/Board.nsf/goto?open&id=BTJRHT6BCBE0.

So far, the PAB has issued three official statements: (1) a statement concerning the death of Breonna Taylor;[110] (2) an analysis of an after-action report produced by 21CP Solutions (a consulting firm),[111] which offered recommendations to the Raleigh Police Department after May 30–31, 2020, protests; in this analysis, the PAB advised the police department to address five items[112] "in order to effectively protect the community during protests that may escalate in the future"[113] and (3) a statement requesting that the Raleigh Police Department engage the PAB in policy changes per the 21CP after-action report.[114]

## The Salisbury Police Chief's Citizen Advisory Board (CAB)

Prior to his relocation to Salisbury, Police Chief Jerry Stokes had begun to assemble a group of residents in Lynchburg, Virginia, to be part of the Lynchburg Police Chief's Community Policing Advisory Group. He retired from the Lynchburg Police Department before the group was officially established, but brought the same concept of collaborating with community members to Salisbury.[115]

The mission of the Salisbury Police Chief's Citizen Advisory Board (CAB) is "to create a forum of citizens and leaders from within the City of Salisbury citizenry to collaboratively address the immediate and future needs of the Salisbury Police Department by researching, planning, reviewing assigned and selected cases or matters, providing advice on department policies, and recommending solutions that will integrate and prioritize the best-case practices."[116]

---

110. Raleigh Police Advisory Board, *Police Advisory Board Statement* (March 13, 2020), https://cityofraleigh0drupal.blob.core.usgovcloudapi.net/drupal-prod/COR10/OEI-PoliceAdvisoryBoard-BTStatement2020.pdf.

111. The report analyzed by the Raleigh PAB is called "After-Action Recommendations for the Raleigh Police Department, May 30–31, 2020 Protests," and can be found here: https://go.boarddocs.com/nc/raleigh/Board.nsf/files/BV8SZL741092/$file/20201110CMORaleighPoliceDepartment-External%20ConsultantsReport.pdf. The Raleigh PAB's analysis of the report can be found here: https://cityofraleigh0drupal.blob.core.usgovcloudapi.net/drupal-prod/COR30/PoliceAdvisoryBoardAnalysis.pdf.

112. The items are the following: (1) evaluate police training with an outside consultant, (2) develop a tactical plan, (3) create a policy to ban the use of expired tear gas, (4) provide accurate and comprehensive budget reporting, and (5) recognize and protect southeast Raleigh.

113. This quote is pulled from page 7 of the Raleigh PAB's analysis of 21CP Solutions's after-action report https://cityofraleigh0drupal.blob.core.usgovcloudapi.net/drupal-prod/COR30/PoliceAdvisoryBoardAnalysis.pdf.

114. *Raleigh Police Advisory Board Demands That RPD Engage the Board in Policy Changes Per the 21CP Report* (March 24, 2021), https://cityofraleigh0drupal.blob.core.usgovcloudapi.net/drupal-prod/COR30/PoliceAdvisoryBoard21CPReport.pdf.

115. Jerry Stokes (Salisbury Police Chief), email message to author, March 23, 2021.

116. *Charter of the Salisbury Police Department Police Chief's Citizen Advisory Board* (2018), 1.

Regarding the Salisbury Police Chief's CAB, Chief Stokes explained:

> Through this group, we are searching for ways to improve community interactions and relationships with the police, but more importantly develop strategies to keep people safe. . .My hope is that this advisory group will advise us on how we can improve relationships, and as we implement ideas, let us know if we are on the right path.[117]

Among the Salisbury Police Chief's CAB functions are providing input on interactions between the police department and community members; reviewing departmental policies and procedures; fostering communication with various disproportionately affected groups; and making recommendations on procedures, policies, or legislation for effectiveness of the Salisbury Police Department and enhance cooperation among members of the community and the police department.[118]

Chief Stokes selected the twenty-five-member CAB with two neighborhood representatives from a grouping of city neighborhoods divided into nine areas based on demographic data analysis (for a total of eighteen members) and one representative from each of the major institutions in the city, such as Livingstone College, Catawba College, and the NAACP. Many of the citizens who have assisted Chief Stokes thus far were involved in a predecessor group, the Salisbury Public Safety Community Action Team.[119]

The Salisbury Police Chief's CAB's first meeting was in February 2018. The CAB meets at least quarterly and provides input on a range of topics. Examples include:

1. Review of the police use of force policy: The Police Chief's CAB reviewed the Salisbury police's use of force policy prior to the summer 2020 protests around the U.S. Following this review, Chief Stokes made some additions to the policy in Summer/Fall 2020.
2. Review of the officer promotions process for input on apparent disparity issues: After the review of this process, some members of the Police Chief's CAB participated in the promotional assessment for the deputy chief, captain, lieutenant, and sergeant positions. The CAB members provided input on the candidates based on interviews they conducted.
3. "After-action reviews" of police department response to situations: One involved an active shooter incident involving college students at a local establishment. The second review focused on civil disturbance response to protests in May and June 2020. The group provided input on possible improvement, and Chief Stokes has updated the group on the police department's progress.[120]

---

117. Jerry Stokes (Salisbury Police Chief), email message to author, January 2021.
118. *Charter of the Salisbury Police Department Police Chief's Citizen Advisory Board* (2018), 3.
119. Jerry Stokes (Salisbury Police Chief), email message to author, March 23, 2021.
120. Ibid.

The chair, secretary, and Chief Stokes jointly organize the Police Chief's CAB meetings. Chief Stokes assisted the Chief of Police of the Town of Spencer in establishing Spencer's Citizen Advisory Board in 2021.

The CAB's charter has a code of ethics that applies to CAB members and the police department. The preamble of the code of ethics states:

> Civilian oversight and advisory practitioners have a unique role as public servants providing a level of law enforcement agency oversight. The community, government, and law enforcement have entrusted them to conduct their work in a professional, fair, and impartial manner. They earn this trust through a firm commitment to the public good, the mission of their agency, and to the ethical and professional standards described herein.[121]

The code addresses personal integrity; independent and thorough oversight; transparency and confidentiality; respectful and unbiased treatment; outreach to and relationships with stakeholders; agency self-examination and commitment to policy review; and professional excellence.[122]

## The Spencer Chief's Citizen Advisory Board (CAB)

The Spencer Police Department's Chief's Citizen Advisory Board (CAB) had its first meeting in January 2021. Chief of Police Mike T. James invited five people to establish the board and aims to grow it to between seven and nine members to best represent various parts of the town. Membership is open to residents and business owners, NAACP members, and clergy. All current members are residents of Spencer, except for an NAACP representative and members of the clergy that pastor a church in Spencer (but do not live in the town).[123]

> The mission of the Spencer CAB is

> to create a forum of citizens and leaders from within the Town of Spencer's citizenry to collaboratively address the immediate and future needs of the Spencer Police Department by researching, planning, reviewing assigned and selected cases or matters, providing advice on department policies, and recommending solutions that will integrate and prioritize the best-case practices. Personnel matters cannot be discussed as they are confidential.[124]

---

121. *Charter of the Salisbury Police Department Police Chief's Citizen Advisory Board*, 1.
122. Ibid., 2.
123. Mike T. James (Spencer Chief of Police), email message to author, April 30, 2021.
124. *Spencer Police Department Police Chief's Citizen Advisory Board Charter*, Article III.

The purpose of the Spencer CAB is to support "a close relationship between the Spencer Police Department and the community," and to be "a means of enhancing police/community relations, communications, transparency, community confidence and trust."[125]

The Spencer CAB does not address police department personnel matters, per state law prohibitions. The CAB is expected to meet quarterly and keep minutes.[126] Currently, the CAB is meeting more often as it becomes established and recruits more members.

The CAB's initial goals are to (1) "foster a positive spirit of cooperation and understanding between the citizens of Spencer and the Spencer Police Department and Town Manager," which will create various ways for officers and residents to "encounter each other in ways that will create understanding and enhance communication" and (2) "to bring guidance and support to the Spencer Police Chief and the Town Manager."[127]

The CAB chose a secretary, chair, and vice-chair in January 2021. COVID-19 precautions have required the first meetings to be conducted via online video conferencing. Chief James sees the CAB as one of many steps to working with all segments of the community and especially for engaging in proactive communication with and developing an understanding with African-American residents. The chief occasionally has similar conversations and meetings with community members and leaders in other areas of law enforcement.

## The Winston-Salem Citizens' Police Review Board (CPRB)

The Winston-Salem Citizens' Police Review Board (CPRB) was established in 1993. The city council asked the existing Public Safety Committee to design the board. Citizens requested the creation of the board in response to a series of events in which citizens felt the police used force excessively. The purpose of the committee is to "act as a fact-finding body in cases involving unresolved citizen complaints against employees of the Police Department."[128]

The CPRB advises the city council's Public Safety Committee and the city manager through the review of citizen complaints. Meeting agendas include reviews of the use of body cameras and the storage of footage. Members regularly meet new police staff members during meetings and discuss policy

---

125. *Spencer Police Chief's Citizen Advisory Board Charter*, Article IV.

126. *Spencer Police Chief's Citizen Advisory Board Charter*, Article VIII.

127. Mike T. James (Spencer Chief of Police), email message to author, April 30, 2021.

128. "Citizens' Police Review Board," Winston-Salem, North Carolina, https://www.cityofws.org/849/Citizens-Police-Review-Board#:~:text=The%20primary%20purpose%20of%20the,a%20Citizen%20Police%20Review%20Board.

recommendations with the chief of police.[129] Citizens can file a formal complaint against the Winston-Salem Police Department. The first step is for the Professional Standards Division to investigate the complaint. If citizens are unsatisfied with the conclusion of the investigation, they can submit the case to the CPRB through the City Secretary's Office.[130]

The CPRB determines the necessity of a hearing and holds hearings that include the submission of evidence, testimony, and findings of fact. Citizens and police employees have the opportunity to tell their version of events and pose and respond to questions from the other side.[131] Both internal and external complaints against officers are considered for hearings. Internal complaints come from employees within the department. External complaints come from citizens.[132] The CPRB compiles the information into a report, which is submitted to the city manager and City Council's Public Safety Committee for consideration. This is the final reconsideration of the complaint. The CPRB does not have the authority to overturn the decision of the city manager and Public Safety Committee.

Annual reports present the number of complaints filed throughout the year. Each annual report lists complaints by type of violation. A single complaint can include multiple violations against more than one officer.

The annual reports detail the types of violations, which can include use of force, courtesy, conformance to laws, abuse of process, unsatisfactory performance, and search and seizure. The 2018 report showed that the CPRB heard a total of ten complaints. Of the total violations within the complaints, eighteen were classified as "exonerated," five were "sustained," and twenty-one were "unfounded." The report indicates that an "exonerated" classification means that the incident occurred, but it was properly and legally handled. "Sustained" means that the incident occurred and that the evidence supports the claim of wrongdoing, while "not sustained" means that there is not enough evidence to prove or disprove wrongdoing. "Unfounded" indicates that the allegation is false, and "open" indicates that the case is still under review. In 2018, no cases were classified as "not sustained," "open," or "withdrawn."[133]

The CPRB heard a total of nineteen complaints in 2020. Zero violations were "exonerated," eight were "sustained," one was "not sustained," fifteen were "unfounded," zero were "withdrawn," and twenty-seven were "open" cases.[134]

There are eleven members on the board. The CPRB's chair and vice chair are elected by the board members. Each member must be a resident of Winston-Salem. Terms last three years, and members can serve two terms. After serving

129. Winston-Salem Citizens' Police Review Board (CPRB), *CPRB Meeting Minutes 2015-2020.*

130. Winston-Salem, North Carolina, "Citizens' Police Review Board."

131. Ibid.

132. Author inquiry to staff contact for City of Winston-Salem.

133. Winston-Salem CPRB, *2018 Annual Report.*

134. Winston-Salem CPRB, *2020 Annual Report.*

two terms, there must be a lapse of one term (three years) before a resident is eligible to serve on the same board. Residents must wait one year after the initial two terms to serve on a different board.[135]

The composition of the board reflects the demographics of the city. One way the CPRB shows the diversity of its members is by identifying them by sex and race or ethnicity on the board's website. As of March 10, 2021, there are three black males, two white males, three black females, two white females, and one Asian male on the CPRB. Residents who wish to serve can contact the mayor's office. The mayor recommends applicants to the city council, which then makes official appointments. Citizens can also directly contact their city council member to express interest in the position.[136]

---

135. Winston-Salem CPRB, *CPRB Rules and Regulations.*
136. Winston-Salem, North Carolina, "Citizens' Police Review Board."

# Appendix B

# Additional Resources

## Links to Webpages of Citizens Police Academies in North Carolina

**Conover Citizens Police Academy**
https://www.conovernc.gov/cpa

**Fayetteville Citizens Police Academy**
https://www.fayettevillenc.gov/city-services/police/about-us/citizens-police-academy

**Guilford County Sheriff's Office Citizens Academy**
https://www.guilfordcountync.gov/our-county/sheriff-s-office/divisions
/community-resource-unit/citizens-academy

**Lenoir Citizen's Police Academy**
https://www.cityoflenoir.com/181/Citizens-Police-Academy

**Mount Airy Citizens' Police Academy**
https://www.mountairy.org/186/Citizens-Police-Academy

**Nag's Head Citizen's Police Academy**
https://www.nagsheadnc.gov/263/Citizens-Police-Academy

**Wilmington Citizens Police Academy**
https://www.wilmingtonnc.gov/departments/police-department/community-programs
-services/citizen-s-police-academy